to
the
top

to the top

JENNA C. FISHER

Russell Reynolds Associates

to
the
top

How **Women** in
Corporate Leadership
Are Rewriting the Rules
for Success

WILEY

Published by John Wiley & Sons, Inc., Hoboken, New Jersey.
Published simultaneously in Canada.

For general information on our other products and services or for technical support, please contact our Customer Care Department within the United States at (800) 762-2974, outside the United States at (317) 572-3993 or fax (317) 572-4002.

Wiley also publishes its books in a variety of electronic formats. Some content that appears in print may not be available in electronic formats. For more information about Wiley products, visit our web site at www.wiley.com.

Library of Congress Cataloging-in-Publication Data:

Names: Fisher, Jenna, author.
Title: To the top : how women in corporate leadership are rewriting the rules for success / Jenna Fisher.
Description: First edition. | Hoboken, NJ : Wiley, [2023] | Includes index.
Identifiers: LCCN 2022056052 (print) | LCCN 2022056053 (ebook) | ISBN 9781119988083 (cloth) | ISBN 9781119988106 (adobe pdf) | ISBN 9781119988090 (epub)
Subjects: LCSH: Women executives. | Leadership in women.
Classification: LCC HD6054.3 .F57 2023 (print) | LCC HD6054.3 (ebook) | DDC 650.1082—dc23/eng/20221118
LC record available at https://lccn.loc.gov/2022056052
LC ebook record available at https://lccn.loc.gov/2022056053

Cover design: Russell Reynolds Associates

To the next generation of women who have set their sights on leadership. Stay the course. Make change. You have the power to improve our world.
And to my parents, Marsha and Ted, whose unconditional love gave me the confidence to realize my dreams and the inspiration to help other people realize theirs.

Contents

Contents

Acknowledgments

I am deeply grateful for the multitude of talented, insightful and cutting-edge thinkers in my life who have helped to make this book a reality. From an idea that first germinated six years ago with my dear friend Mary Abusief, the incredible writer Sara Leslie and my gifted colleague Heather Blonkenfeld, as we brainstormed together around a conference room table in my Palo Alto office, imagining how we could use our collective wisdom and experiences as professional women to benefit the next generation.

Fast-forward five years to the middle of Covid in 2021, when I decided to use the two hours I had recaptured every day by not having to commute to instead interview 50 incredible women around the globe who are shining examples of how we can get women to economic parity with men. I then had the unbelievable luck of being connected to the fierce and whip-smart Lisa Roth and Alanna Stang at Well Said in New York, who served as my True North and got me to synthesize my findings and taught me how to engage with LinkedIn as a tool to help spread my gospel. I so admire you both: thank you.

When I pitched my fantabulous CEO Constantine Alexandrakis on this book concept early in 2022, he was immediately enthusiastic and supportive, realizing that it gelled perfectly with RRA's goals of DE&I and improving the way the world is led. From there, marketing genius Amy Scissons, RRA's Chief Marketing and Communications Officer, partnered with me to expertly shepherd me through the publishing labyrinth, which had heretofore been a mystery to me.

My writing companion Samantha Marshall beautifully wove together our stories of these diverse women into a cohesive whole in record warp speed, always ensuring my voice was coming through. It bears noting that a few months into this book-writing process, Sam was diagnosed with cancer and had to undergo surgeries, chemotherapy and radiation alongside our interviews; and yet, she never stopped believing in the message of this book and stuck by my side until the manuscript was done. To say she was courageous and tenacious in the face of enormous stress and physical discomfort would be an understatement of monumental proportions, and I am forever grateful to her for never giving up, even on the really dark days. (And I am overjoyed to report that she has made a full recovery.)

Susie Sell, my London-based marketing colleague who was always literally nine hours ahead of me – and figuratively, always even more on top of things, is an absolute gem. Susie, we are so incredibly lucky to have you here at RRA. From telling me what to wear to photo shoots to reassuring me that we had everything under control, your talents seem to be truly limitless. This book definitely would not be possible without your expertise and innumerable talents. I owe you a knickerbocker glory.

To my many RRA partners around the globe – I wish I could list all 180 of you by name here! – who checked in with me, believed in this book's message, and proactively and graciously opened your Rolodexes to introduce me to the most incredible professional women you know. Robert Voth, Ulrike Wieduwilt, Harald Kringlebotn, and so many others – your generosity and trust are what our firm is all about. And to Aimee Williamson and Dee Fitzgerald for your incredible research, and, of course, Tina Shah – I am so privileged to work with cutting-edge thinkers who care so deeply about this important mission.

To Gena McAndrews for working scheduling magic to somehow shoehorn all of these interviews onto my already overly committed calendar – I truly could not function without you by my side. To Catherine Schroeder for helping me diligence and research so many of our interviewees – you are always at the ready to help me be prepared, so thank you for being so caffeinated and ready to spring into action when I need you. To my other partners Amy Hayes, Chris Faralli, Tuck Rickards, Nick Roberts, Jim Lawson, Clarke Murphy, Justus O'Brien, Justin Cerilli, Paul Ottolini - thank you for letting me poll you on book title ideas, cover designs, and myriad other things. To Clemens Frischen-schlager and his team – thank you for designing more book cover concepts than I can count – I am so delighted and impressed with your creativity and your end product – I really appreciate how you "got" me in all of my pinkness. To Abby Zeitlin, Callie Bennett, Bea Constable, Miranda Thurtell and the rest of my beloved FOP team, who never stopped cheering for me – thank you for being the best colleagues someone could ever ask for – I'd trust you with my life.

And to the many, many women who enthusiastically jumped in and said, "Yes!" when I asked them if I could interview them, hear their life's stories, and who openly and candidly shared their struggles, fears and successes with me. I am humbled by how impressive all of you are; if the next generation of women can learn only a tenth of what I have had the privilege of learning from you, they will be so much better off for it.

And a huge thank you to my wonderful publisher Shannon Vargo at Wiley who believed in this book's mission and message from the first moment – the way you made me feel so supported is something for which I'll always be grateful.

Finally, to my devoted, loyal, insightful, and hilariously funny husband Colin, who is as much of a feminist as I am – thank you for always putting my career at the top of your list of priorities.

I know you believe in this book as much as I do, and I appreciate that more than you can know. And to the two lights of my life, Morgan and Peyton: you are the part of my legacy of which I am most proud. I wrote this book in large part because I want you to grow up in a world that is even better than the one you inherited, and it is my hope that you will each continue our tradition of repairing the world, little by little. Keep being your awesome, unique selves – you are perfect just as you are. I love you with everything that I am.

Introduction: A Post-Pandemic World

A few times a year, I am asked to talk to MBA students at leading business schools around the country about how to manage their careers. In 2022, I was speaking to a group of undergraduate students at a leading school, and at the end of the session we held a Q&A. In addition to their intelligence, savviness, maturity, and poise, what really stood out to me was that many of the women students asked me essentially the same questions:

> "How can I make my voice heard – and make it to the top?"
>
> "How should I negotiate my compensation, even when it feels awkward?"
>
> "How many boxes do I need to check before starting my own company?"
>
> "Is it *really* possible to have both a career *and* a family?"

These were some of the brightest and most accomplished women from all around the world, and yet the undertones of their questions made me realize – at the age of 21 – that they were already looking down the barrel towards their futures and questioning whether they could "have it all," whether they could succeed when they looked at how few women were at the top table today, and when they had seen so many talented women permanently step out of the labor force.

After everything that women have accomplished and the myriad ways in which things are so much better for us than they were only a generation ago, we still have some of the most talented and fiercest women questioning if they can rise to the highest ranks within corporations. It struck me that businesses and society are failing this generation of young women. We are so far from where we need to be in terms of gender parity.

As a partner at one of the top global leadership advisory firms, I have had a mission to get women to 50–50 representation at the highest levels of management and boards in corporate America, but for specific reasons I will break down in the chapters to come, it's not happening nearly fast enough. In the United States, women comprise 51% of the population; 47% of the workforce; and 70% of high school valedictorians; and yet (at the time of writing) Russell Reynolds Associates' research shows that only 9% of CEOs in the largest 100 companies in the S&P500 index are women.[1] There are, in fact, about the same number of women CEOs in the S&P500 as there are CEOs named James or Michael.[2] Over my 20-plus-year career, I have met thousands of eminently qualified and intelligent women with long lists of educational and career accomplishments who have struggled to make it all the way to the C-suite. It is a loss not just for these individuals, but for society as a whole.

So how do we get there?

As I thought more about the Q&A session with the undergrads, I realized that while some of the answers to these students' questions hadn't changed since I was myself a college student, some of them had – and drastically.

It made me think of a conversation I'd had with Christa Quarles in September 2020, a few months into the global Covid-19 pandemic that, as I write this, is still playing out around the world. Christa had been recently appointed as CEO of the global software company Alludo. She was a client-turned-friend who also happens to be a neighbor of mine in the suburbs of San Francisco. On a scheduled break between Zoom calls, we decided to throw on our sneakers and take a power "walk and talk," to discuss my concepts for this book. It was a welcome chance to check in with each other in person.

At this point the dramatic shift from office life to working remotely from home was still relatively new. Christa and I started comparing notes about how our professional lives had changed. Suddenly we had a luxury we'd craved for years: time. As working moms who were no longer spending two hours a day commuting in our cars to and from the office, we were able to see our children more and have family dinners together for the first time. And although I was working intensely, bouncing nonstop from meeting to meeting virtually, networking and writing reports from my craft-room-turned-home-office, I was getting more work done than ever.

It goes without saying that the pandemic resulted in untold personal and economic losses for millions. But some light was emerging from the darkness, and we were just beginning to see it.

"Christa, I can't imagine ever going back to the old way of working. I am getting a lot more accomplished than when I was sitting at my office desk. Am I crazy to think that this should be the new way forward?" (Little did I realize then that it would be more than two years before I would return to the office.)

"3,000 percent!" said Christa. "The pre-2019 office is a relic. Why would anyone ever want to go back to that artifact of a factory organization? In a digital economy we can talk to someone face-to-face from anywhere, we know how many deal closures you've made, and none of it is predicated on whether you did it inside an office. Who cares if you're picking your kids up from school at three o'clock when you're crushing it!"

This mindset was a complete change for Christa. Charismatic, with an acute intellect, a razor-sharp sense of humor, and endless reserves of energy, she'd ascended to the highest ranks in the male-dominated software industry, and before the pandemic had been attending every function, event, and leadership forum in her industry, flying across the country and around the world to meet customers and colleagues.

"If you'd asked me in 2019 whether I would ever become an advocate for remote work, I would have absolutely said no. I've got to corner that person in the elevator. I've got to stop people at the coffee machine. Being an in-person leader was part of my special sauce. I loved getting in front of that town hall meeting. I fed off the energy of it all."

Long before the lockdowns, many Alludo employees were already working hybrid or remotely in different locations across the world, from Ottawa to Tokyo, to Frankfurt, to Austin and Seattle. But it was an ad hoc approach that left some on the sidelines. The pandemic changed that, establishing a new normal that created the opportunity for a more inclusive work environment that took into account different approaches. The tech industry has historically been a man's world where the most vocal – or perhaps the tallest – get recognized. But Christa began to appreciate the individuals who were quietly getting it done.

"Do you think the universal remote work situation was empowering to certain personality types who may have been overlooked in the past?" I asked her. "And to women in particular?"

"The thing about remote meetings with larger groups is that everybody's Zoom box is the same size," Christa observed. "It enables you to go around the room, or I should say the screen, and ask people's opinions. It engenders a kind of equality. Everyone's viewpoint gets represented and it becomes much harder for a few people to dominate."

As Christa spoke, it occurred to me that we were in a rare moment in history where we could completely reset the workplace culture in a way that would be more inclusive. We were undergoing the biggest shift in how we work since the Industrial Revolution. And with more leaders like Christa at the helm who were reshaping organizations to allow for more multidimensional ways of working, communicating, and thinking, a long-overdue change could be here to stay. Through the forced circumstances of the lockdown, many of us were given our first delicious taste of what a healthy work–life balance could be. It showed us that this way of operating wasn't just new, but better – and it could potentially become the launch pad for more women to reach the highest level of corporate leadership. This was our chance to finally break through, in what Arianna Huffington described as a "Third Women's Revolution: The first one was giving us the vote; the second was giving us access to all jobs in the top of every profession; and the third one is women saying, 'We don't just want to be at the top of the world, we want to change the world, because the way the world has been designed is not working.'"[2]

Fundamental to this revolution is a workplace environment that's more authentic and welcoming to all genders, where leaders empower and enable the best from individuals, whether they are new moms pumping breast milk at home before jumping onto the next client call, a young, newly "out" gay Black man struggling to find his voice in large group meetings, or a "sandwich-generation" person in need of a more flexible schedule to care for an aging parent with dementia. It is about taking into consideration the life circumstances of an individual – male, female, or non-binary – and giving the trust and work style options necessary to bring out their best as professionals and create a pathway for them to rise in the organization. In short, it is nothing less than a transformation of the world and its social values to welcome all genders and backgrounds.

But it's not just the changing working practices that made me optimistic for women. The global pandemic helped to rewrite the rules on what it means to be a great leader. The seeds of this change were planted long before Covid-19 hit, but there is no doubt that the pandemic accelerated the shift.

We are living through a moment in history when the old definitions of success and what it takes to lead are giving way to something that is altogether more collaborative and more inclusive. Gone are the days of the "hero CEO," who mimicked a wartime general to exercise absolute authority and control. Today's world is a much more complex world, as events like Covid-19, and issues like sustainability and digital disruption, force every business to rethink their business models, their operations, and yes, their leaders.

We are seeing a demand for leaders who cultivate a kind of compassionate command. A study of thousands of direct reports published in the *Harvard Business Review*[3] found that, during a time of crisis especially, there was a strong desire to be led by individuals who could "pivot and learn new skills; who emphasize employee development even when times are tough; who display honesty and integrity; and who are sensitive and understanding of the stress, anxiety, and frustration" that people were feeling, listening without judgment or recrimination.

This is good news for women. Among top leadership characteristics, according to Pew Research, women were perceived to be more compassionate, empathetic, and able to reach compromise. Women also rated higher in terms of resilience, integrity, taking initiative, and showing a willingness to learn – traits highly valued not just in a crisis, but in the new and inclusive workplace that must define the post-pandemic world.

For example, an analysis of 122 speeches[4] of men and women leaders during the pandemic also showed that women were more likely to use terms of compassion, reassurance, and unity, compared with war analogies and threats to keep their populations in line. The gentler, more sober messaging worked. Studies even found that countries with women leaders during the pandemic had better outcomes, including fewer Covid cases and deaths than nations led by men, while states in the U.S. with women governors fared better in terms of Covid deaths than those with men holding that office.[5]

So the evidence is in that with traits like compassion, empathy, the ability to listen, mentor, nurture, and collaborate, it can be argued that women leaders have certain advantages. That is not to say men can't also possess these qualities, or that women don't possess so-called male traits. Great leadership surpasses gender. But there's a reason why more male C-suite leaders are brushing up on their "soft skills." It is what their employees want.

The table was set for change by the seismic global events of 2020 to 2022, and there has been widespread recognition that there is a better way to manage our world. But gains from this moment could so easily be lost if organizations don't become more intentional about building flexibility into the workplace and codifying a hybrid model that allows people of all genders to channel their whole, authentic selves into their professional lives. If these dynamic times have taught us nothing else, it's that our well-being as workers and future corporate leaders matters.

That's why I am writing this book. Where we are now – in any industry – isn't good enough. At the current pace, there is no way women can achieve parity in my lifetime, or even my daughter's.[6] According to a 2022 study by the World Economic Forum, at the current pace of change, it will take 132 years for women to reach economic parity with men! Personally, I feel a deep sense of urgency to build on the strides that we have made during the pandemic, before they are displaced by a reflexive and destructive return to the "old" normal. *We must not go back.*

My perspective on this subject has been honed from two decades of experience recruiting people to the highest ranks of companies on behalf of the global leadership advisory firm Russell Reynolds Associates, where I am a managing director and head of the CFO practice.

Throughout my career, I've had the good fortune to get to know countless inspirational and successful individuals. It has given me a front-row seat into the cultures of a broad cross-section of industries, particularly how supportive and equitable companies are, or are not, towards their women leaders in terms of pay, promotions, and access to opportunities. This book chronicles the journeys of some of those talented and resilient women – across geographies, industries, races, and functional specialties – who have charted a path to the top, with some unique and often surprising insights on what they believe it will take to clear the obstacles for the next generation of women leaders.

Executive Search: A Primer

Executive search is an often-elusive industry, so let me take this opportunity to tell you a bit about it.

Search is like any other professional services field like law, investment banking, or accounting in that our clients pay us to represent them in the market. We are paid a fee (never contingent) to go out and to find the very best people for them to consider for their next CEO, CxO, or board role. Think of us as matchmakers for the corporate world, linking the best people to companies and executive roles. Our counsel and market intelligence are invaluable to clients, who often need to decide between promoting someone internally versus hiring from the outside, as both tangible and intangible skills and benefits must be considered. Because most of us who are search professionals end up loving it and doing it for a lifetime, the same person in our professional milieu can serve as a client one moment, a candidate another, and then also just be a member of a shared professional community. People often ask our advice about compensation, the reputation of other executives, and how to navigate and negotiate delicate and dynamic professional situations. We get to know these individuals' partners, their children, what motivates them, and what keeps them up at night. We are honest with them because we know that the same candidate or professional contact might become a client in the future. I think of my privileged role like that of a proverbial priest or rabbi to the professional world. Although we aren't saving lives in our work, when you think about the most profound changes most people must manage – short of marriage, divorce, birth of a child, death of a loved one, buying a home – taking a new job ranks right up there.

The women's stories in this book have taught me that we have reached a critical juncture. I have advocated for women my entire professional life. But never in my career have I been more convinced that the time to advance the path to parity is now. As Winston Churchill once said, "Never let a good crisis go to waste."

On the coming pages, I will outline how we can permanently build a more inclusive way of working into corporate culture to launch more women to the highest echelons of business. In Part One, I will set the scene in detail to describe the moment we are in, how we got here, and how we can leverage what we now know into real transformation. This book is anchored in both proprietary research, including RRA's own data on the specific leadership traits companies are looking for, as well as insights on how well women perform against them. Taken together, these data points prove that women are standing on the most solid foundation for success that we have ever seen.

In Part Two, you will learn how bold actions and radical shifts in mindset, both for individuals and at the organizational level, can accelerate the pace of parity and finally close the gap. Beyond the data, I will give you detailed examples and stories of individual women leaders – from Nike, to Walmart, to Atlantic Records, and dozens of other global organizations – who have already done it and are doing it every day.

What you will *not* read on these next pages is a list of instructions on how or what to change within yourselves. The pages that follow will put the onus on organizations – *not* on the individual – to change and keep women on a sustained path to success. After all, the reason that women constitute less than 10% of CEO spots at the largest 100 companies in the S&P 100 isn't because women aren't working hard enough.

Instead, by the end of this book, I want you to recognize, embrace, and leverage all the many strengths that you likely already possess. My promise is that I will never implore you to bend, lean, or adjust to outside expectations. From countless books and TED talks, you've already heard enough lectures. It is the narrative that must change, not you! By all means, evolve, educate, and develop your skills. Just know that you already own the tools: my goal is to help build your confidence to use them. The women who inspire me most are successful precisely because they have embraced who they are and achieved that critical balance not just for themselves, but for those they have mentored, developed, and empowered along the way.

Which brings me back to Christa. She was among the leading architects of this redesign of work as she onboarded dozens of new associates from diverse backgrounds during the pandemic. She brought on impressive leadership resulting in a C-suite that was 50 percent women. She created a safe space for honest feedback, setting up a channel with thoughtfully worded survey questions where all employees could anonymously give their candid views on how they felt about their work conditions. (Oh and by the way, 95 percent of respondents said they wanted to continue with remote work, and the number of women who said they wanted to go back to the days of physically going into an office could be *counted on your fingers* across the entire company.)

Coincidentally, her survey results aligned with my own research from July 2020, where I polled 200 of my clients, "Once it is safe to do so, how many days a week would you like to return to the office?" Only men said they would want to go back five days a week. Women overwhelmingly preferred remote work or some sort of hybrid model.

Christa then analyzed the three main reasons why her associates might want to gather together in a physical location: a desire for in-person action, "to see the whites of someone's eyes" even if just for one day out of the work week; the potential creative benefits of collaborating in a group; and a place to go, "a work pod" that offers a better environment to focus in than, say, a 500-square foot apartment in Tokyo shared with a musician boyfriend (who plays drums). Whatever these employees' motivations for changing out of their yoga pants, Christa carefully crafted a hybrid work model that included flexibility, trust, and a set of metrics for quantifying actual productivity and not just how many hours are logged in front of a computer screen. Because when individuals, including leaders, are held accountable using objective measures of success, it is often the quiet achievers who shine.

"I have long seen women get judged on experience and men get judged on potential. That's why we need to get clear on the right way to measure. It's not the input, it's the output we should be focused on," Christa explained.

As we finished our walk and stretched on the front steps to my house, I wondered aloud if Christa and I were alone in our observations, or if more women in the highest ranks of corporate America were also having this epiphany.

"Christa, would you say these past few months have made you a stronger leader?"

"Absolutely! I didn't start my career as a fully formed human being. All that alone time during Covid gave me the opportunity to orient myself. It made me realize that you only live once, and making deep and authentic human connections rose to the top of my list. I just didn't have it in me anymore to have a conversation that wasn't pure, vulnerable, and direct."

My conversation with Christa reminded me that the old, Industrial Age models of in-office work were developed by men, for men, at a time when women weren't even allowed to vote, much less pursue a career. Despite all the talk around getting women to the top, the corporate environment has never been designed around women's needs. Again, this is our moment. But it's no longer about trying to get a seat at the table that wasn't made for us – it's about working together to build a better table,[7] with new definitions of success and what a leader looks and sounds like. It's time to throw out the old, patriarchal characterizations of success. We need to demonstrate the truth that women have what it takes to be amazing leaders not by emulating men, but by being true to ourselves.

As I sat back down in front of my computer to dial into my next video call, I felt even more resolved to populate the board rooms and executive offices of the world with more women like Christa.

I have always believed that if more women governed nations, there would be less war. If women wielded equal economic power to men, there would be less domestic violence, because financial empowerment would give women the strength to leave. Economies around the world would be bolstered if half their country's inhabitants didn't step down prematurely, unable to maximize the full potential of their careers. And if more children saw examples of highly successful women, both men and women would be empowered to follow their passions, which would ultimately make the world a happier and safer place.

Let this be the beginning of a new era where women take their rightful and proportional place among the leaders of the world. Let us collectively uplift and support each other to create a society where each individual's talents are captured and deployed in ways that are most rewarding and recognized. If you are a young woman embarking on your career path, believe in yourself and have the confidence to get what you deserve. If you are running a company and managing people at work, read and learn how to better support and inculcate the kind of widespread change and thought leadership that will uplift and improve our professional lives. And if you are parents, set the example to help your children be their best selves and get them to 50–50, one little girl and boy at a time.

We still have a mountain to climb before we achieve true parity in business. But it's also clear that we now face the opportunity of a lifetime to fast-track progress and accelerate the stubbornly slow trajectory of change. Women are now standing on the most solid foundations for success than ever before. It's time to grab this opportunity with both hands.

PART ONE

The Third Revolution

CHAPTER 1

The Myth of Progress

As society sees what women can do, as women see what women can do, there will be more women out there doing things, and we'll all be better off for it.

—Ruth Bader Ginsburg

In 1983, when NASA was helping astronaut Sally Ride prepare to become the first American woman in space, their team of engineers put together a care package of all the things they thought she might need while living in zero gravity some 200 miles above the Earth's surface. Included among these items were tampons.

Scientists weighed them and considered carefully whether the right kind for the confined space would be deodorized or unscented. NASA is extremely particular about what is allowed to go onto their spacecraft, where every square inch of capacity counts, so getting it right was a big deal. They even tied the tampons together with their strings, so they wouldn't scatter and float away. Their next question: how many?

"Is 100 the right number?" one of the physicists famously asked her.

"No," she replied, deadpan. "It is not the right number."[1]

One. Hundred. Tampons. For a six-day stay on the Space Shuttle. Thoughtful? Very. Absurd? Absolutely!

Yet the team persisted. (I am sure it won't be much of a surprise to most of you that the NASA staffers fretting about Ms. Ride's period needs were all men.)

"What if you get stuck up there?" they asked. Ms. Ride assured them she was quite certain she wouldn't need 100 tampons, even if the mission were to go a few days overtime. If it took much longer, menstruation would be the least of her workplace problems on the space shuttle *Challenger*.

I heard this story as I was on my treadmill, listening to an NPR podcast by comedian Marcia Belsky. She sang a song about it that went viral, and I laughed so hard I nearly fell off the machine:

I'm walking tall/I feel so proud/Then I see a man running panicked through the crowd/He's holding a large bag. I think, what can this be?/And then he hands 100 tampons to me.[2]

Myopic Lens

Ms. Ride's experience demonstrates that, no matter how well intentioned, when an organization lacks diversity, when the decision-makers see a situation through their own limited lens, things can easily go wrong. And, for centuries, that lens was white and male. The result has been an entrenchment of corporate cultures that arose out of the needs, assumptions, and expectations of that one group. It's perhaps one reason why most C-suites are still overwhelmingly populated by men. According to RRA's research of the largest 100 companies in the S&P500, men make up 72% of executive leadership teams, versus 28% for women. This means that there are 69% fewer women in executive leadership teams than we should expect based on the gender-split in the US workforce as a whole.[3]

The current infrastructure remains out of date. That's not to say companies necessarily set out to exclude women. I would say that most are now trying to be inclusive. But lack of understanding and limited perspectives at the top can create a multitude of barriers for women and any other underrepresented group that cascades down and across every function of the business.

It's also why the progress women have made in the corporate world has been, by and large, a myth. There is a widely held misperception that there is already a 50–50 split in the workplace. You would think so because women are graduating from college at higher rates than men, and there are more women than men with postgraduate degrees. During the 2018–19 academic year, more than 1.1 million women earned a bachelor's degree, compared with fewer than 860,000 men, according to the Brookings Institute.[4] That's 74 male graduates for every 100 women, across all subject areas. At the entry level, women and men are more or less at par, according to recent gender gap research by McKinsey.[5] But in the highest-earning fields like finance and technology, women remain woefully underrepresented.

Figures like these may account for the false sense that achieving gender parity at the top is just around the corner. But those who are paying attention know that those ratios change precipitously as one looks higher up the corporate ranks. At the management level, the proportion of women drops by a staggering 10 points to 38%, and it continues to dwindle at each stage along the executive career track. As of June 2022, there were only 44 women running Fortune 500 companies.

And in the world of finance, where I spend the vast majority of my time as a leadership advisor, just 18.2% of CFOs are women. Yet the proportions rebalance massively when you look further down the corporate ladder. According to the US Bureau of Labor Statistics, published in September 2021, 62% of accountants and auditors are women, and 55% of financial managers are women.

"That collective stumble on the first step up the corporate ladder suggests that over the next five years, one million women in corporate America will get stuck at the entry level while their male counterparts move into promising career paths," note McKinsey partners and study authors Kevin Sneader and Lareina Yee. "That is equivalent to nearly 25 Major League Baseball stadiums full of women."

Something needs to change. Although many companies promote an array of progressive values and targets, the numbers show a different story. Women are not ascending to the top positions in corporate America.

For all the strides made by the tech industry, and with all the leading-edge technology we have at our disposal to measure productivity and enable remote work, this flexibility is far from baked in. Even in the tech start-up space – an industry that prides itself on its progressiveness and has had opportunities to build inclusion into its models from the beginning – any movement towards parity has stagnated. Sheryl Sandberg's legacy when she left Meta in 2022 as COO was impressive, with more women in higher executive ranks. This champion of women in the workplace not only encouraged women, she recruited and promoted them to top positions. But the exit of arguably the most powerful and high-profile woman in Silicon Valley to focus more on family and philanthropy, however understandable, means we have one less formidable figure in the highest ranks to inspire us. Consider that the highest positions at Big Tech firms like Alphabet, Apple, and Amazon are still dominated by men. Big Tech, based on its influence in the world, should be leading on gender and diversity. It's not. Only 4.8% of the top 150 technology firms were led by women by the end of 2020 – the same percentage as in 2018.[6]

"The snail's pace of progress for women leaders in Silicon Valley is worse than disappointing," Nicole Wong, a deputy chief technology officer for the Obama administration and a former Twitter executive, told the *New York Times* when Sheryl announced her departure.

We can no longer afford to be complacent or accept the status quo. At the current pace of change, it could take another 150 years before women achieve parity in corporate leadership. That means not even our daughters or our daughters' daughters will experience the benefits of a world that is as accommodating to women as it has been to men. It's time to change our approach.

For starters, companies need to radically revamp their recruitment, development, and retention practices. While many women opt to leave the workforce to start or raise their families, that only partially explains the figures.

There is often so much focus on what women should do differently to ascend to the highest ranks. The lists of "don'ts" throughout the years has been long: Don't show too much emotion. Don't be too assertive. Don't be vulnerable. Don't laugh too much. Don't talk about your family. Wear makeup, but not too much. Look pretty, but don't be too distracting. Over recent decades, the list of rules for women looking to succeed at work has bordered on the absurd. A PricewaterhouseCoopers (PwC) dress code from as recently as 2015, for example, mandated that women must wear hose and heels!

Clearly, it's not women who need to change. It is the actions and attitudes of companies and their leadership teams. Organizations need to proactively accommodate, bend, adapt, and expand to include us all, and the change needs to be formal, systemic, and subject to accountability. For too long, women have been bearing the burden of change when it should be the other way around.

Think Pink

When I first started Russell Reynolds back in 2002, a senior partner at the firm made the astute observation that I love pink. My clothes, my nails, my accessories, my pen, my desk art – all had rosy hues.

"That's a lot of pink, Jenna. You might want to tone that down a bit," he suggested.

"This is who I am," I told him.

If anything, after that remark, I doubled down on my color. Years later, as I became one of the top-performing partners at the firm, the same man came up to me and said, "I think I owe you an apology. That pink thing seems to be working out for you just fine."

"It's not women we need to fix; it's the way that all of us perceive and react to and interact with women that we need to fix," Mary Ann Sieghart, author of *The Authority Gap* and former *Times of London* political columnist, put it in a recent *Redefiners* podcast. "So it's not really for the woman to change the way she is, it's for the rest of us to change how we behave towards women." That applies to organizations as well as individuals. And it starts at the top.

The Power of Three. . .or More

According to Petra Axdorff, CEO of BAMA Gruppen AS, Norway's leading distributor of fruits and vegetables and one of that region's oldest trading companies, "Every company needs at least three women on the management team reporting to the CEO. Only one, and the woman becomes captive to the majority and their way of thinking. Just two and they are still isolated and less able to influence the whole. With at least three, there can be a diverse team that will be better for everyone. Three is enough to start to build that critical mass and break through."

It's still not enough. It needs to get to 50–50, and having only three should never be accepted as the status quo. But when you reach that magic number, the whole dynamic at the top table shifts. It's no longer the lone female. She becomes less of a unicorn. Other women, particularly those who aspire to lead, can suddenly see themselves in that role when there are three.

Getting more women to the top is critical. But even that is not enough. Ultimately, *every* leader, regardless of their gender, needs to be actively moving their organization towards parity. Only then will the wheels really start to turn.

"A boss is everything," shared pioneering newswoman Lesley Stahl in 2022, on RRA's *Redefiners* podcast.

Lesley, who has won 13 news and documentary Emmy Awards, broke through as a national news anchor and reporter decades earlier because the man who hired both her and Connie Chung was "totally, 100% committed to affirmative action. He was not going to let us fail. The commitment of the boss is so vital for anything to succeed."

That level of support looks like a senior leadership team that demonstrates humility, acknowledges their own limitations, takes the time to learn about their people, and shows that they value what each person brings. They are genuinely curious about cultural differences, and how the unique experiences of a woman or minority employee might shape how they work, and the perspectives they bring. Leaders truly interested in making progress on inclusion must also be comfortable with transparency and be prepared to acknowledge the feedback about what is and is not working. And, critically, we need leaders who recognize that the entire organization needs to make gender parity a priority and are willing to invest in addressing biases and overhauling the outdated structures and programs that are holding women back.

"It's one thing to say you want more women in the C-suite," Mindy Grossman, former CEO of WW International (Weight Watchers), told me. "It's another thing to provide the support that's needed to help them achieve and continue to move forward."

Mindy, who previously served as CEO of the Home Shopping Network, and as a senior leader at Nike and Ralph Lauren, has done just that. One of the many reasons she has been ranked among the top women in business by the *Financial Times, Forbes,* and *Fortune* has been her vocal and proactive championship of equity at all levels of the workplace and beyond, having promoted and mentored countless women onto her top leadership teams. Women like Mindy at the helm can make a huge difference. But unless the entire organization makes diversity an investment priority, we will never achieve parity at the top.

"If you really want to attract and retain the best and most diverse talent entering the workforce, you have to invest in the support mechanisms that are going to empower people to be in those jobs and excel," Mindy continued. "Ultimately it will save business dollars and create opportunities that will help the economy."

Burning Out

While in some ways the pandemic leveled the playing field for women in terms of minimizing time spent commuting and on the road traveling away from family, there is also a real risk that without the right support structures, we could find ourselves going backwards, not forwards.

According to the International Labor Organization,[7] 54 million women worldwide left the workforce during the pandemic. It is perhaps of little surprise given how much Covid blurred the lines between work and family, and how women were often disproportionately impacted in terms of the care burden. In fact, research conducted at RRA shows that nearly 33% of the executive women of color who left a job during 2021 did so because they needed the flexibility to "work from anywhere." (Only 3% of white male executives made the same choice.)[8]

During the pandemic, women were quick to step up to the plate to support their teams. A McKinsey study reports that women leaders were twice as likely as men to spend time each week helping team members navigate work–life challenges. These leaders were also the ones driving well-being and DE&I initiatives.

Yet going above and beyond the day job, carrying out work that, while critical, often goes unnoticed, can come at a heavy cost. RRA research showed that twice as many women executives than male executives cited burnout as a top reason for leaving their jobs.

Clearly, if companies do not address employee demand to balance work and family life, especially for underrepresented executives, they risk reversing any progress (and investments) they have made towards parity at the top.

But the challenges of retaining top leadership talent, particularly women and underrepresented/excluded groups, predate the pandemic and aren't only attributable to this circumstantial burnout. While most men in our RRA research cited better pay and career advancement for leaving jobs, leadership, talent management, and cultural components were major factors for underrepresented groups. Women specified the need for "a different 'kind' of leadership" and reported wanting to feel more valued by their organization as major reasons for moving on.[9] In other words, it behooves organizations to do much more to attract and retain women and underrepresented/excluded groups because inclusion sits at the heart of retention. Whatever the benefits being offered, leaders and leadership-track talent must first feel valued as individuals, and that is not just some quick fix. Those in top decision-making positions must walk the talk of diversity, equity, and inclusion in ways that are viscerally felt. And this includes tackling the unconscious biases that continue to hold us back.

Backwards in Heels

Regardless of seniority, unconscious bias is always in play, especially for a Black women. Stanford University professor of neurosurgery Dr. Odette Harris experiences varying degrees of it almost daily. At a national surgical conference, the doctor and academic was mistaken by one of the other attendees for the waitstaff as she moved around the hotel ballroom to stretch her legs.

This gentleman, presumably one of the organizers, proceeded to give her instructions about how to set up lunch.

"I'm at the table," she told her professional counterpart. "I am not making the table."

Odette was stung, but the realization that she had been stereotyped, not seen, by one of her peers, even though she'd been at the same table as he was all morning and had participated enthusiastically in the conversation, did not come as a shock. It happens all too often. At another conference, where she was a keynote speaker, with "Odette Harris, MD," written on her attendee badge, a man asked her, "Oh, so you're from Maryland?" because, shockingly, it made more sense to him that she would have her home state abbreviation on her lab coat than she could be a medical doctor?! When she was a visiting professor receiving an award at another prestigious medical school, she was stopped by security no fewer than 15 times in three days, asking to see her identification card.

"It's just so deflating," Odette shared. "Imagine if you had to hold the burden that, for every interaction you had, someone had to validate your existence."

Unconscious and conscious biases are pervasive in her world, yet somehow she is expected to bounce back from each slight. Odette is well aware that other neurosurgeons don't get looked up and down by patients and then quizzed on their credentials. She estimates that, about 90% of the time, patients ask her where she went to school or Google her, then proudly inform her that they now believe she is competent for the job and title she holds.

"The year I graduated in neurosurgery, only seven other women graduated in the entire country. We didn't have the same extensive network that the male graduates enjoyed. All eyes were on us, judging us as we carried the load, without the recognition that, although we all appeared to be doing the same work from the outside looking in, there were tons of differences."

Odette likened her entire residency to the famous Ginger Rogers quote: "I did everything Fred Astaire did, only skipping a beat backwards, and in heels."

Odette's experiences reminded me that whatever societal expectations and constraints limit us as women in the workplace, for women of color the challenges are exponentially greater. And if Odette is facing these biases as one of the country's top neurosurgeons, what challenges are women facing further down the corporate ladder?

RRA's research paints a bleak picture. In a 2021 global survey, 63% of C-suite executives said senior leaders at their organization showed a bias or favoritism towards those like them. And a further 61% agreed that it is easier for men to get promoted than women (regardless of their capability and performance). While it is encouraging that C-suite leaders are clear-eyed on DE&I challenges – acknowledging a problem is often the first step towards solving it – this data should be taken as a clear signal that more must be done to root out and change patterns of behavior that undermine DE&I at every level.[10]

Success Roadmap

In addition to recognizing, acknowledging, and addressing cultural issues, senior leaders need to provide specific tools and pathways to get you to where you need to go. They should spell it out, offering more flexible career paths to accommodate different goals and priorities – ways to grow and ascend into every role or function that include vertical, lateral, and cross-functional entry points and progression routes, because it doesn't always need to be a straight line to the top. And as Amy Bunszel, EVP of software giant Autodesk, told me, "You shouldn't have to sprint every mile of your career. Sometimes it is okay to just walk for a bit." The more pathways, the more room there will be for those with different experiences and career timelines to come into the C-suite.

Beyond the career roadmap, training, and development, companies need to do a better job of extending benefits to those whose life circumstances don't fit the conventional nuclear family unit, where co-parents can share childcare duties, for example. Single mothers, single fathers, or someone who is childless but the only caregiver of an aging or ill family member need additional support so that they can bring their whole selves to work. I will talk a lot about flexibility on these next pages – a key theme of this book – but intentionally setting up tools and structures for inclusivity is about much more than simply allowing talent to manage their own schedules or occasionally work from home. There needs to be a broader understanding of where a woman is on her life's journey so that she can use her knowledge and talent in ways that enhance the business without depleting her energy and attention as a mother, daughter, or caregiver.

Outside the Lines

When Heidi Locke Simon, a trailblazing partner formerly at Bain & Company's San Francisco office, lost her husband in 2010, she faced the dual challenge of having to build her career as the sole breadwinner and raise her young daughters, one of whom was still not yet born. As a widowed professional she experienced countless moments in her career when she felt very much alone and faced unfathomable choices either to take a risk that could propel her career or to leave her children potentially stranded without the level of childcare with which she felt comfortable.

"It's not like divorce, when at least you know there will still be a parent to take care of your child if something happens to you," noted Heidi. "There are more and more single parents like me who don't have any family support infrastructure."

Heidi made the choice to bring her daughters with her to her first board meetings in Europe after the pandemic because she didn't want to risk Covid travel restrictions locking her down in a country for weeks at a time without her girls. On another occasion, Heidi passed on a trip to Cuba because, as sole parent, anything that put her at risk had implications not just for her, but for her daughters.

"I don't care what the advantages of travel to a place like that are right now, I am not going in person. Sorry," Heidi recollected.

Building a village as two working parents does not present the same challenges it would for women like Heidi. Things that, as a co-parent, I might find annoying or slightly upsetting, like a flight delay, "can be terror-inducing," she shared with me, "and in my kind of career it happens a lot."

Of course, Heidi has her network of friends, relatives, child-care providers, and other school parents. She's been intentional about building relationships with people she trusts. She's sought out reciprocal arrangements and built up her "favor bank." But in those unavoidable, last-minute situations, she needs a backup of four or five people who would be willing to drop everything at the last minute, "and you can only go back to the well so many times."

"When it's one adult and children involved, and you are trying to battle and manage everything by yourself, it is different," Heidi explained. "In that situation, you can't do it all yourself, but some women feel this perfectionistic pressure to do everything."

A little understanding about the challenges faced by women and other individuals who live outside the usual lines can go a long way towards alleviating that pressure, empowering them to focus on building their careers. Expectations need to be more elastic as organizations do more to accommodate more diverse talent. Instituting benefits like family leave and making it available to all groups can help. Organizations can also ensure equity by providing access to flexible working arrangements for all employees by taking into account their potential caring responsibilities for family, loved ones, their personal mental health needs, even pets.

It's a balanced approach my business school professor, at the Wharton School, organizational psychologist Stewart D. Friedman, has been advocating for decades. He points to the mounting evidence within organizations like Target, UnitedHealth, the US Army, and others, that "four-way wins" – improved performance at work, home, in the community, and for the "private self" – empower both men and women at all career stages. Allowing them to "experiment with new ways to fit together the pieces of their lives"[11] leads to better business results because employees are better able to bring their most focused and engaged selves to work. In fact, as Stew has told me many times, we need to retire the phrase "work–life balance" because the punctuation in between implies a tradeoff that simply doesn't exist. Maybe we can't have it all at any one point in time, but we sure can have more of it all than we realize.

Through practicing initiatives that make room for our whole selves, we learn that "work and life don't always have to be a zero-sum game," wrote Stew back in 2012 in a *Harvard Business Review* article entitled, *"'Having It All' Is Not a Women's Issue."*[12] The more that individuals are able to practice leadership in all areas of their lives, the more productive and less stressed they feel. "And their performance at work improves even as they devote less time and attention to it and more to other aspects of their lives. It sounds paradoxical, but it's what we observe time and again: when people focus more of their attention on the things that matter, they are more efficient, engaged, and productive."

Organizational leaders have been exposed to more holistic ways of thinking about talent development for decades. Ideas that have proven to benefit business and lend themselves to a more gender-balanced workplace are nothing new. And yet getting widespread adoption of these practices remains an uphill slog.

Just Doing It

Thoughtful, incremental changes won't get us to parity fast enough. Organizations also need to set more ambitious diversity and equity goals for themselves. For those who think it can't be done, Norwegian infrastructure giant Mesta AS is an inspiring case study. In September 2019, when Marianne Bergmann Røren was brought in as CEO, the company, which provides maintenance on critical infrastructure, and builds roads and bridges through some of the most challenging terrain on the planet, had no women on its management team and was performing poorly. Marianne decided to restructure and set a goal of having women comprise 50% of the management team. But she didn't just want any women. She wanted serious talent. "I did not believe the bullshit that there weren't enough women available for the top positions," she told me. And to the many recruiters who said they couldn't find her those capable women her response was, "Well, you're just not looking hard enough."

Marianne wanted other types of diversity too – not just in terms of gender or race, but also functional expertise. Mesta's previous leadership team consisted solely of white male engineers. To bring a fresh perspective, Marianne sought candidates who had general experiences from other types of businesses and backgrounds. To find the best people, she removed names and other clues about the gender, ethnicity, and backgrounds of each job candidate, and focused purely on the experience and skill sets each potential hire could bring. As it happened, more than half of the most appealing resumes belonged to women. Marianne also took some risks, hiring some people who had not yet checked every box in their careers, but experience to date and backdoor referencing revealed they were true "A" players. If they did not perform, "you do what you normally do with the top management group. You take them out and bring someone else in," Marianne told me. "It's not diversity for diversity's sake."

Marianne's diversity strategy worked. After years of limping along, group revenue rose from approximately $460 million in 2020, immediately following the extensive reorganization, to $540 million in 2021. The company is now expanding into rail and other areas of infrastructure. Marianne believes the diverse approach is what shook Mesta out of its stagnation, and she's pushing hard for the rest of the organization to become 50–50, including blue-collar jobs, by making it one of the KPIs for her hiring managers. "If you don't hire women, you won't get your bonus checks," she has told her management team.

Julie Greenwald, chairwoman and CEO of Atlantic Records Group, took the same approach when she became record label president almost two decades ago. She restructured the business and brought in more women to lead her management teams, which now comprise more than 50% women, which is unheard of in the music industry.

"Maybe I can't change the world, but I can change my plot of land," Julie told me. "If we all took care of our little pieces, the world would be a much better place."

IKEA is another Scandinavian company that has proven it can be done. In the 2000s, the Swedish home furnishings giant counted only eight women among its 200 leaders! In 2019 its holding company the Ingka Group committed to 50–50 gender balance in all countries where it operates. As of fiscal year 2022, 46% of all leaders were women, and 51% of all co-workers were women.

In 2018, the company joined the Equal Pay International Coalition (EPIC) to hold itself accountable to an external international body, and it established the IKEA Group Diversity and Inclusion Approach, which features a program to raise awareness of unconscious biases. The IKEA Women Open Network, or IWON, was also set up to provide a forum for gender equality issues, where potential biases in policies and rules are openly discussed, along with suggested improvements for redressing gender imbalance. IKEA also implemented worldwide six-month family leave policies, decoupling traditional gender roles in having and raising children. It's a wholesale approach that goes far beyond ticking the boxes.

"Building an inclusive IKEA is more than a recitation of our values – it is taking thoughtful and habitual action," read a 2022 LinkedIn job post by IKEA North America's first chief diversity officer, Stevie Lewis. "Practicing inclusion and making it authentic requires an open mind, intention, and application of learned behavior. Creating an inclusive environment is a condition precedent for a successful diversity strategy. Authentic inclusion changes our lens, expands our perspective, and magnifies our purpose."

Petra Axdorff, who left IKEA to helm BAMA in 2021, was among the senior leaders implementing the policies to reach gender parity in her previous role as CEO and CSO of IKEA in Spain. The Swedish-born executive held various senior international management roles at IKEA, which began its parity journey at the top, cascading the policy deliberately and methodically down throughout the organization and across functions to include every level. It was a snowball effect, but getting that ball rolling began with the education, training, and accountability of IKEA's leaders. There had to be a wholesale shift of mindset.

Petra's main mission as leader was to empower her people. She tapped people to become project team leaders who didn't necessarily fit the mold of management or see themselves in that role, but whose diverse experience led to better business outcomes. It soon became obvious that the more parity and diversity in the teams, the more competencies are brought to the table, and the better the decision-making, productivity, and performance.

"The traditional criteria of whom can be a leader is wrong," Petra told me. "I wanted to prove that diverse leadership delivers."

As CEO of BAMA, a much smaller organization with around 3,000 employees, Petra wants to find that next level of enabling others through diversity. As leader, she sees that inclusive approach as good business.

"When I empower people on my team to think and act, I have hundreds more brains I can lean on besides my own."

Her vision is to build a business comprising self-confident, proactive individuals with the capacity to reach the right decisions through open discussion and a blend of perspectives. This type of organization, she believes, would essentially run itself. Mixed teams would take initiative rather than waiting for permission to act. Petra believes this is a more democratic, less hierarchical leadership style that is strategically inclusive. She knows it can't happen without gender parity.

We may not have yet fulfilled this vision, but Petra remains optimistic. She believes we are at a moment in history where it may be possible to speed the pace of gender parity across industries. As in the United States, in central Europe, she notes, well over half of university graduates are women, and they are entering a job market where there is a severe talent shortage. "If a business intends to grow, it will be hard not to recruit and retain more of these women at the top."

"That scarcity will play into our hands because you cannot avoid 50% of the talent pool," Petra told me.

But for those who do not take serious actions to enable better outcomes, she's in favor of government regulation or mandates to set some parity protocols for businesses. Because, as a mother to three teenage daughters, getting there sooner rather than later is a deeply personal ambition.

"It may be time for government to force the speed. Because, despite everything, we are not moving fast enough."

* * *

Your Path to the Top Checklist

Fix the leaky pipeline. Too much potential talent is being lost along the way. Organizations need to take a hard look at their recruitment, development, and retention practices and apply more equitable talent management to retain their women leaders and keep them on the path to success

Follow the rule of three. At a minimum, companies need three women on the management team and on the board. Only one, and she becomes captive to the majority and their way of thinking. Just two and they are isolated twins and less able to influence the whole. At least three enables more diverse points of view in the room.

Reaching the right number isn't enough. It's about supporting those women through policies, programs, and strategies that help them succeed, and building on that success through support mechanisms that are going to empower people to be in those jobs and excel.

Be more elastic. Allow diverse talent whose career progress doesn't fit the usual parameters to experiment with new ways to fit together the pieces of their lives. This more flexible approach will lead to better business results, because employees are better able to bring their most focused and engaged selves to work.

It starts at the top. Leadership-track talent must first feel valued as individuals, above and beyond any benefits, rewards, training, or talent development, and that is not just some quick fix. It starts at the top. Those in the top decision-making positions must walk the talk of diversity, equity, and inclusion in ways that are viscerally felt.

Create support networks. An informal board or kitchen cabinet focused on finding solutions for underrepresented talent will help them feel less alone and more empowered.

Equal, not same. Parity is also about recognizing that individuals have different lived experiences. These diverse perspectives are a plus for business but, because of systemic challenges, some may need more flexibility and support to do the same job.

As a leader, be curious. Demonstrate humility, acknowledge your own limitations, take the time to learn about your people, and show that you value what each person brings. Do not make assumptions about anyone else's lived experiences.

Create a career roadmap. Spell it out, offering more flexible career paths to accommodate different goals and priorities – ways to grow and ascend into every role or function that include vertical, lateral, and cross-functional entry points and progression routes, because it doesn't always need to be a straight line to the top.

Force the speed. Set more ambitious diversity and equity goals because the world cannot wait another 150 years to reach parity. Recruit the best talent from the whole population by experimenting, doing blind searches, and entertaining different business backgrounds and skill sets. And tie diverse recruitment goals to job performance indicators. Because if you can't find the right women, you are simply not looking hard enough.

CHAPTER 2

Meeting the Moment

"And once the storm is over, you won't remember how you made it through, how you managed to survive. You won't even be sure, whether the storm is really over. But one thing is certain. When you come out of the storm, you won't be the same person who walked in. That's what this storm's all about."

—Haruki Murakami, *Kafka on the Shore*

I'm an early riser, usually up with the sun. But on September 9, 2020, I awoke in total darkness. Mornings that time of year are usually crisp, bright, and sunny, with the first pink rays piercing through our bedroom blinds, so I wondered for a moment if it was still the middle of the night. I walked over to the window, which faces east over the San Francisco Bay, and scanned for some glimmers through the gloom. Nothing.

It was disorienting, even dystopian. I later learned that it was one of those freakishly unpredictable events – the combination of a thunderstorm a few weeks before that had ignited about 100 wildfires spanning from Santa Cruz all the way up to Wine Country. The fires had raged for weeks, producing thick blankets of smoke that eventually mingled with the city's fog. First the sky turned black, and then the color of a Halloween jack-o'-lantern. It is now known as "Orange Day."

That day the sun disappeared felt like the end of the world. It seemed to augur something sinister and gave me a sense of foreboding that is etched in my memory. For me it came to symbolize all the disturbing news of the global pandemic, the perpetual uncertainty, and the economic devastation so many were facing. And yet it's true what they say about it being darkest before the dawn.

We are still finding out the full extent of Covid's impact, good and bad, but as the weeks and months unfolded after Orange Day, I had the growing sense it might be possible for humankind to make another great leap forward because I saw the positive changes occurring in the lives of my clients and candidates. Again, what we are living through in real time is another kind of Industrial Revolution. Or, more accurately, we are experiencing the beginnings of a Workplace Leadership Revolution that could dramatically accelerate the closure of the gender gap in organizations around the world. We're not there yet, but we are on the precipice of something profound.

That's the thing about cataclysmic events throughout history. For all their wreckage, for all their undeniable human suffering, they can also lead to advancements as we navigate our way to the other side. During World War II, for example, women *became* the workforce as men went to war, taking factory jobs and building skills never before considered "feminine." And much as society tried to return Rosie the Riveter to the kitchen, there really was no going back.

We also invented. Glamorous Hollywood actress Hedy Lamarr, upon learning what was happening to Jews in Nazi concentration camps, used her considerable mathematical engineering genius to co-create a "frequency hopping" device to evade Germany's attempts to jam the signals of the US Navy's radio-controlled torpedoes. Her extraordinary achievement (for which she never received full credit in her lifetime) not only helped the Allies find and sink German U boats, winning the war, it was foundational to the nascent field of wireless communication. Her invention put the world on a path that would ultimately lead to the development of GPS, Wi-Fi, and Bluetooth technology.[1]

What brightened my outlook more than anything during the pandemic were the many conversations I had with other women leaders, and the opportunities I was given to witness their wisdom in action. This was a moment in history that revealed a special kind of strength consisting of resilience, persistence, alacrity, and empathy. Across all industries and realms, we were getting it done.

Woman of the Hour

When I think of this blend of grit, authenticity, and passion, I think of Mary Dillon, who was named CEO of Footlocker in 2022, becoming one of just a handful of women to lead a Fortune 500 company. Before that, she led cosmetics retail giant Ulta Beauty through the unprecedented business headwinds of the global pandemic. The mother of four, who waitressed and cleaned houses to put herself through college, was forced to temporarily furlough 30,000 of her 44,000 workers as she digitized the business, slashed inventory, and streamlined its global supply chain.

The company was in deep crisis, as was the case for many retailers in 2020 when a record 12,200 brick-and-mortar stores closed.[2] Had she not taken this bold action, Ulta would not have survived. But she forewent her own base salary indefinitely and personally donated $500,000 to the Ulta Beauty Associate Relief Program. As chair of the Retail Leaders Industry Association, she also became the champion for millions more retail workers, intensively lobbying the federal government to include economic relief for the retail industry in the first stimulus bill to help sustain those who had temporarily or permanently lost their incomes.

"We need companies to survive. We need people to go back to work," she told media outlets. "And so, we are counting on making sure that the bill that passes really thinks this through and gives us options in terms of liquidity and capital."

As the news rolled in and retail faced yet more closures, many of them permanent, there were a lot of opinions about how to survive. This CEO listened. But she also trusted herself enough to take the information and make the right call, including going all-in on e-commerce, with innovations like an online digital mirror so customers can try on makeup shades, and increasing wages for employees serving that side of the business. Then, using her authentic voice to cut through the noise, she communicated her convictions clearly to bring key stakeholders along with her.

The business results of Dillon's leadership were extraordinary. Sales grew from $2.7 billion in 2013 when she started at the company to $8.6 billion by March 2021 when she left (on par with pre-pandemic levels), and they were on their way to breaking sales records by the third quarter of that year. Known for her steady hand, she is so well regarded by Wall Street that Footlocker's shares shot up 19% on the news of her appointment.[3]

Mapping the Traits

Leaders like Dillon exemplify the shifts we see in leadership across the world. The seeds of these changes began around a decade ago, fueled by new societal norms and employee expectations, as well as issues like technology disruption, and now sustainability. But it's also true that the chaos of the pandemic hurled us into the future at an accelerated pace. And now we find ourselves in the midst of what can only be described as a leadership revolution.

"We are seeing a move away from a world that was much more tangible to a world that's much less certain, where there is a need for greater agility," explained my colleague Dee Fitzgerald, a Sydney-based consultant at RRA and one of the architects of an RRA study on the future of leadership. "It is no longer about managers delegating and instructing. It's about leaders who can create purpose and meaning for others. It's less about 'me' and more about what I can do to include my broader stakeholder group – my employees, my communities, my customers."

So, as the world shifts on its axis, what exactly does it now mean to be a great leader? And what does it take to get to the C-suite?

RRA's research shows shifts in four key domains:

- **Thinking**

    It used to be that leaders were prized for their intellect and the accurate analysis of the situation in front of them. Today, it's more about anticipating the needs of the future, and understanding the organization in full technicolor. It's about being able to navigate the complex and multidimensional ecosystems within which organizations operate, a capability we refer to as "systems thinking." As another colleague, Aimee Williamson, the Sydney-based global leader of our Assessment capability and co-author of the study put it, "It requires stepping beyond the here and now to connect the dots and identify patterns to look at the whole system rather than the sum of the parts."

- **Delivering**

    This particular domain, which refers to executing and getting results, used to be about "command and control, being on top of the data, giving clear direction to others, and making sure everything is done exactly the way you want it to be done," Aimee, who is also an industrial psychologist, explained. It then shifted to a more delegative environment with clear measurements or KPIs to monitor the performance of the team. But today, "delivering" is about being able to adapt in the absence of certainty. "Instead of counting the widgets, delivering refers to being agile and comfortable with a world in flux," she said.

- **Leading**

   Again, we've largely moved from a more militaristic approach to leadership, taking charge and directing, to a more engaging, motivating, and collaborative style that enables and empowers. Aimee explained, "Today's leaders seek to find overarching meaning and purpose for their people, giving them something to connect to. It is a less transactional and more purpose-driven and inspiring way of engaging."

- **Influencing**

   Finally, the domain of influencing used to emphasize the relational aspects of networking in order to build connections, knowledge and get the job done. Today, having influence as a leader refers less to your own journey and more about building an inclusive community, leveraging your EQ and empathy. "It's about drawing out and amplifying the voices that are different and getting to a more innovative answer," said Aimee. "It is one of the reasons why we are seeing such a demand for diversity on boards right now."

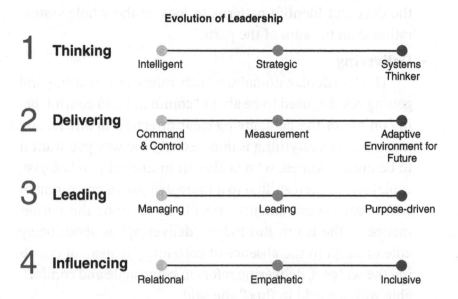

Evolution of Leadership

1 Thinking
Intelligent — Strategic — Systems Thinker

2 Delivering
Command & Control — Measurement — Adaptive Environment for Future

3 Leading
Managing — Leading — Purpose-driven

4 Influencing
Relational — Empathetic — Inclusive

This isn't just theory. When RRA analyzed the position specifications that our clients have us craft to explain the specific skills they are looking for in their next executive, we found that mentions of terms related to systems thinking, adaptability, being purpose-driven, and inclusive leadership traits increased significantly between the two time periods we studied: 2002–2006 and 2018–2021 (see graphic). This analysis shows clearly that not only do these skills matter, they are in growing demand by leading organizations around the world.

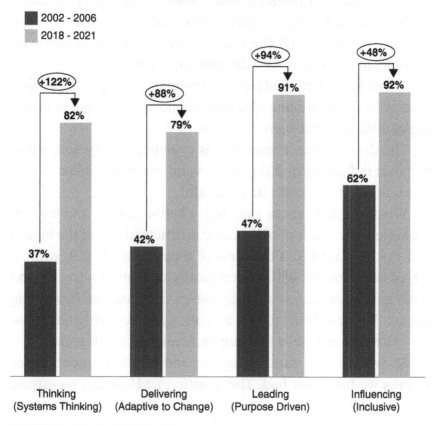

Increasing importance of critical leadership skills
% of role specifications containing terms

2002-2006 N = 1221; 2018-2021 N = 2036

Source: RRA, proprietary analysis of role specifications (2022).

Subtle But Significant

A recent *Harvard Business Review* article called it the "Era of Exponential Change."[4] Covid "laid bare a new normal" that consists of relentless, pervasive, and exponential change requiring an entirely new way of leading that moves past the old linear – one might even say patriarchal – ways of thinking.

Clearly, the debate about the differences between the sexes has raged for decades. The purpose of this book is to not wade into this hornet's nest. Again, by no means am I suggesting that the most desired leadership traits are exclusive to women. But, through RRA's partnership with Hogan – generally regarded as the leading workplace personality tool, which uses a range of scales to understand the values, styles, preferences and even derailers of executives – we do have some insights.

When RRA compared men and women on Hogan scales that predict the most in-demand leadership traits, we found no meaningful difference between the sexes.

The data is clear. Leadership is evolving rapidly and, when it comes to leading in 2023 and beyond, women possess just as much of what it takes to be successful.

Whatever differences exist today between men and women are largely the result of old social constructs (think of the classic doll that is placed into the arms of a two-year old girl, while a boy of the same age will stereotypically be handed a truck), and those small details, over the course of decades, can have a big impact. Men can learn to be – and often are – empathetic. These are behaviors and skills that can be developed and learned.

So women are standing on the most solid foundation for success we have ever had. The question is: How can we ensure companies and our society help to propel women forward by having the right infrastructure in place to ensure their success?

"We need a new form of leadership, better equipped to navigate this unprecedented kind of change," wrote Aneel Chima, director of Health and Human Performance at Stanford University, and Ron Gutman, a healthcare technology entrepreneur and Stanford lecturer. Their conclusions came from conversations with top global organizational leaders ranging from Toby Cosgrove, former CEO of the Cleveland Clinic; to Doug McMillon, president and CEO of Walmart; to Bret Taylor, former Co-CEO of Salesforce; and one especially formidable woman: Halla Tómasdóttir, CEO of the B Team, investor, and co-founder of Reykjavik University, who came close to winning Iceland's 2016 presidential elections. These luminaries came up with the concept of "Sapient Leadership," a combination of wisdom, discernment, vulnerability, openness, and authenticity. They concluded that these were the very qualities needed to navigate this tumultuous period of disruption because they inspire the "trust and psychological safety that drives shared learning and intelligence, resulting in enhanced collective performance and leading to a better future for all."[5]

Tómasdóttir – whose B Team members include Arianna Huffington, former president of Ireland Mary Robinson, Sir Richard Branson, and Marc Benioff, to name a few – describes this leadership approach as a rejection of the old model of leader as "individualistic hero." Today's ideal leader must be willing to bend and change according to the needs of the organization, not the other way around.

Put simply, it's about setting aside ego and putting others first to empower them to excel. "What this crisis has shown us is that the leadership style of 'I know it all' is not a good leadership style for this moment or any other challenge we are going to continue to face and need to deal with collectively, collaboratively, with compassion, and with care," said Tómasdóttir.

Which of course inspires this question: If women leaders have these adaptive traits in abundance, why should the women CEOs in the Fortune 500 be part of such a tiny club? Why would there not be many more Mary Dillons when industries are crying out for this balance between emotional intelligence and clear-eyed strategic thinking?

In talking to hundreds of executives over the past two years and delving into why some businesses thrived despite the pandemic and its fallout, the common thread among the responses was that the best leaders take command with compassion. These leaders understand that the way to navigate through the darkest days is to focus on human capital. Many people I spoke with cited the humanity and care of women leaders. Often, though not always, she is a mother, who takes the same thoughtful approach to raising, supporting, and educating her children so they become successful adults. She invests in the well-being of everyone in both her family and the organization, gaining trust through transparency and fostering deeper relationships with team members and cascading the vision and values to all levels and functions of a business that provides not just a job but a shared sense of mission.

The shift to purpose-driven business and the push to meet sustainability goals requires a different set of skills than what was needed five years ago. Corporations will not survive unless they go beyond pure profit and participate in serving the greater good. So command and control are out. Collaboration, humility, transparency, and authenticity are in.

This new dawn has been a long time in coming, but the confluence of epic and disruptive global events, particularly the pandemic, means there can be no turning back.[6]

Critical Care

For Dr. Odette Harris, the neurosurgeon we met in Chapter 1, letting her staff and colleagues feel seen and heard is integral to the
way she leads. The ability to communicate with and engender the
trust of the members of your team is critical in any organization.
But when you are performing brain surgery, that seamless, swift
decision-making and action is literally a matter of life and death.
So I was intrigued to find out how Odette, who is also the director
of the Brain Injury Program for the Stanford University School of
Medicine and serves as deputy chief of staff for rehabilitation at
the Veterans' Administration Palo Alto Health Care System, builds
those relationships. I learned that they do not happen by accident.

"In the operating room the physician has the inherent ability
to command the scene," Odette explained to me. "But I think it is
beholden on us to really leverage our skills to make everyone feel
whole and part of the team."

The power of soft skills

More than ever, companies need leaders who are good with
people. Our research with faculty members from the Harvard
Business School and Imperial College London looked at how
expectations on C-suite executives were change. And we found
that strong social skills are now in high demand—whether
that's the ability to listen, excellent communication, or playing
well and empathizing with others.

Our analysis identified four reasons behind the shift:

1. Firm size and complexity

As organizations become more complex, top executives must be
able to coordinate specialist teams, manage a multitude of relationships with outside partners and stakeholders, and communicate

powerfully with their employees. For all those tasks, it helps to be able to interact well with others.

2. Information-processing technologies

As companies use technology to automate routine tasks, demand is growing for "human skills," such as judgment, creativity, and perceptiveness—skills that computers don't have (at least yet). In technologically intensive firms, leaders have to respond to unexpected events and manage conflict in the decision-making process, both of which are best done by managers with strong social skills.

3. Social media

Historically, CEOs weren't constantly in the public eye. But the rise of both social media, which can capture and publicize missteps instantly, and platforms like Slack, which let employees discuss their bosses in real time, has changed this. And as commentary on their decisions becomes instant, poor communication, even in the eyes of just a handful of people, can have big consequences.

4. Diversity, equity, and inclusion

Organizations are, rightfully, putting ever greater importance on diversity, equity, and inclusion. Leaders who can perceive the mental states of others can more easily interact with various employee groups, make them feel heard, and represent their interests. More importantly, they can nurture an environment in which diverse talent thrives.

There's an inherent hierarchy in medicine, "and that deferential assumption you are good is yours to lose," Odette explained. There is also a comfort level with colleagues who have trained alongside you for extended periods. But as a woman, particularly a Black woman in this field, nothing can be taken for granted. That level of respect needs to be reinforced with an authority leavened by humility and a sense of humanity – something this doctor has practiced since medical school.

"Over time, I think you bring about a sense of collegiality by always being respectful, always being kind," Odette observed. "And then because it's a hospital, it's like a small village. People talk and your reputation, for better or for worse, gets carried."

Odette already has a reputation not just as a brilliant surgeon and medical researcher, but also as an organizational leader. Yet it's those unseen moments that many other leaders would not necessarily consider – outside those critical bedside and operating table exchanges where she builds her credentials. Before a surgery, for example, she takes the chance to huddle "like at the beginning of a game" with everyone from the anesthesiologist to the nurse whose job will be to wipe her brow or pass a scalpel. Odette described it as a "timeout procedure" that simply acknowledges everyone's presence and role. Then there are moments throughout the case that are less critical, when Odette chats with a nurse or technician about their lives beyond the operating room.

"There are points in the procedure where you can actually step out of that intense focus and conduct a conversation without putting the patient at risk," she told me.

Even if it is an especially complicated case, there will always be those moments of calm. It could come at the end, when the patient's incision is being closed and all vital signs are stable. The conversation is intentional, but the flow is organic and authentic. With impeccable timing, as everyone exhales, she'll clear out the tension by making a witty remark and follow up by asking them about something personal, like their plans for the weekend. She'll also share a little about what's going on in her own life. Then, as everyone is walking out of the OR, she'll thank them one by one for their great work and dedication, specifically recognizing what they did well. They may seem like small gestures, but it helps form a sense of community even among surgeons and specialists who aren't regularly on the same rotation or, as Odette puts it, "in the trenches" with her.

Odette finds many ways to pull people into the fold. She never misses a colleague or staff member's birthday. She'll be the one to buy the cake, get the card, and gather everyone around the office for the "surprise." As the leader, she hosts holiday and summer parties at her home, and takes them out of the workplace setting for coffee or lunch a few times a year.

Why does it matter? Because this personal approach eases communications and allows team members to be more vulnerable with her, ultimately leading to improved capabilities.

"There is a lot of bravado in our field," Odette observed. "A resident who might not know something may be reluctant to admit it. You hear them say, 'Oh, I've done this a hundred times,' which of course is not even possible by that stage in their careers. But if you already have a personal connection with somebody and have had a glass of wine with them, and you understand them beyond the surface level, they can open up about their insecurities. I do whatever I can to promote a deeper bond. That way they feel less judged, and that creates the opportunity for more teachable moments, which ultimately add up to better clinical outcomes."

Hardcore Strategy

There are business benefits to this kind of relationship building.

"Make no mistake, there is also a hardcore strategy behind my use of those softer skills," Odette continued. "Building those relationships and fostering that collegiality has helped us all to achieve mutual goals."

Odette, who, in 2018 made history by becoming the second Black woman neurosurgery professor in the US, began running three programs at Stanford, and has since expanded her domain to 16 programs, which required significant support and funding from senior administrators and donors. In business terms, what she has accomplished in her field is akin to a CEO successfully expanding a portfolio of companies or brands.

"If you can get people to trust you, understand your competence, and to actually see you as a human and an ally, it goes a long way," Odette observed. "Like begets like, so people always want to feel as though they have something in common with you."

Realizing the inherent challenges of being a woman and a minority in a hierarchical and traditional power structure like neurosurgery, Odette went beyond what was expected, meeting in person with the various leaders related to her programs on a quarterly basis, instead of relying on occasional phone calls to discuss issues as they arose. The result? She is as admired, trusted, and respected by the most senior leaders in her field as she is by the nurses and orderlies who work shoulder to shoulder with her in the patient wards.

"I didn't have to do that, but it was an opportunity for us to sit and chat. I used my soft skills so they could get to know me as a person. Because, when I am giving you the strategy for the department or discussing budgetary requirements, they are more likely to listen when they feel like they know where I am coming from. In my experience that is just as important in establishing credentials as giving a presentation and listing all my successes."

A New Dawn

At the end of every conversation I've been having with female leaders as clients and candidates, I make a point of asking them whether they are optimistic about the future of women in the C-suite. Does our new way of working, and the effectiveness of "compassionate command" on retention, morale, and business outcomes, give them hope for a more equitable workplace? The answers are mixed. But they all have agreed that this new way of working is good for women and families, and if it is good for them, it will be good for everyone.

* * *

Your Path to the Top Checklist

Cut through the noise and trust yourself. As women, we are well-positioned to meet a moment in human history where a new form of leadership is needed. As you lean into inherent traits like empathy, open yourself to diverse points of view, and embrace a willingness to learn, you will find you are well-equipped to navigate this unprecedented change.

Kindness and compassion are smart business strategies. And the numbers prove it. Flexibility for both frontline workers and office associates enables people to be more focused, which pays dividends in terms of productivity and retention, because, overwhelmingly, it is what they want.

Communicate intentionally and proactively. There is a hard-core business strategy behind the constant conversation. It builds allyship and buy-in to your goals. Whether it's about having a human moment and sharing news of your child's baseball team, or getting in front of business-related issues, an open channel builds trust and respect, leading to improved outcomes for the performance of the business and individuals.

It's not just a woman thing. Building more compassion and flexibility into your business and leadership strategy benefits men too, enabling them to be better partners and parents, and enhancing productivity overall. A rising tide lifts all boats.

The small details can be huge. Engaging in the moment on a personal level, checking in, creating space for team members and associates to breathe, providing resources for mental health, and so on are noticed and appreciated, engendering loyalty. They also happen to be common facets of the way great women leaders lead.

CHAPTER 3

Digital Empowerment

Technology has the ability to be the great equalizer and so we really need to focus on this as a society, and on how we do this the right way.

—Jacky Wright, chief digital officer, Microsoft

Donna Morris was less than a month into her role as Walmart's chief people officer when the retail giant saw its first stateside case of Covid. Late on a Friday night, Donna was in her rental apartment in Bentonville when she got the call to come to the company's Emergency Operations Center (EOC) in northwest Arkansas early Saturday morning. Located in the company's home office, the EOC is where associates physically and virtually gather to deal with any kind of emergency, whether a natural disaster, a fire, or, in this case, a pandemic. With her bags and boxes not yet unpacked from her recent move from California, Donna immediately pivoted to crisis mode, preparing to head back to the offices in the early morning with no idea what she was about to face. When she arrived at the massive complex, she found her way to the situation room in the back, where about 40 colleagues were studying an entire wall of digital screens. The monitors were live streaming data from Johns Hopkins that showed the number of Covid cases across the country and the virus's rapid, state-by-state projected trajectory.

"We immediately started thinking about how we were going to run our stores, distribution, and fulfillment centers while protecting the 1.6 million associates who worked for us in the United States, and that started a domino effect of what my job became," Donna told me.

The monumental challenge was that the majority of their associates weren't office-based who could go home and work from their laptops, although those who were office workers did. But the business would not function without its frontline associates, who interacted the most with the general public. With Donna and her team playing a key role, Walmart responded to the rapidly evolving situation by consulting with the CDC and with state and local health experts, implementing cleaning and sanitizing protocols and providing personal protective equipment. They immediately introduced an emergency leave policy, waiving the attendance policy for anyone who chose to stay home during that period of uncertainty (regardless of Covid or quarantine status), or for those required to quarantine, and provided up to 26 weeks of paid leave for those who contracted the virus. And they made all their associates eligible for funds from their Walmart Associates in Critical Need Trust, regardless of tenure.

It was a Herculean feat of logistics that required a 30,000-foot understanding of a situation that was in constant flux, along with a deep sense of the individual needs of their associates and the customers they served. It required leadership that blended empathy, strategic thinking, and decisive action. But in addition to responding swiftly to the immediate and obvious needs that would keep the doors open and associates empowered to work, Donna soon turned her attention to ways her workforce could benefit beyond the pandemic. The innovation for the workforce needed to be focused on the front line. The team worked to develop "Me@Walmart," an app that would support greater associate access to scheduling and work-related benefits, along with tools for on the job. Ultimately, Walmart provided more than a million frontline workers with a digital device to support work and life, including the ability to have more command of their own schedules.

"There will be optionality, and that will allow people to engage on a different level. Hopefully more companies will offer these benefits so parents don't have to feel conflicted, an associate can take care of an elderly parent, receive health treatment, or they simply take a break if they feel stressed out."

While Walmart does not have a hybrid model of working for all associates, the company is focused on providing flexibility for associates. Ultimately, Walmart is enabling associates to be more engaged and focused on serving customers and members, which is paying dividends in terms of productivity and retention.

Flexibility = Productivity

There has been an awakening to new ways of working and leading that has swept across industries, regardless of role or rank. Even CFOs, who used to spend weeks of their year flying into and then schlepping around New York and Boston visiting investors, have told me that for 90% of their interactions now, everything is so much more efficient over Zoom. The genie is out of the bottle, and most businesses will need to enable remote work or some hybrid model of remote and in-person if they want to retain their best talent.

Nearly all the companies that used to be staunch believers in everyone being in the office together have now internalized that if they adhere to those old norms, they are going to miss the boat on the top talent in the market. Employees have options, and they want balance in their lives. They now know rationally that they don't have to waste hours and days of their lives driving and flying when, in many cases, their work can be accomplished just as successfully over Zoom. We have collectively proven it. And I predict that Millennials will continue to challenge our old assumptions and ways of doing business. By and large, Millennials aren't willing to sacrifice like my generation did – and they know that they don't have to.

And we have the numbers to prove it. Now that they have had a taste of it, 72% of workers say they prefer a flexible work model, according to a global survey of 9,000 knowledge workers conducted by Slack.[1] The workforce solutions platform ADP Research Institute[2] found that 67% of employees said they felt more empowered to take advantage of workplace flexibility, compared with 26% before the pandemic. This would seem to make workplace flexibility a critical tool not just for employee retention, but productivity. The 2021 State of Remote Work Report by videoconferencing technology company Owl Labs[3] found that this was overwhelmingly the case, with 90% of employees reporting that they were as productive, if not more, working remotely. So, when leaders like Donna take pains to introduce more flexibility into the lives of their workers, it's not just about being a nice boss. It's good for business.

Anytime, Anyplace

On March 10, 2020, as I was driving to work, I received a call from my assistant, telling me that people were feeling apprehensive about coming into the office. The coronavirus had recently arrived on the West Coast and this news put them on edge. I somewhat begrudgingly agreed to the temporary closure of my firm's office, which I was running at the time, thinking that it would be just a few weeks of working from home before we'd go back to life as we had always known it. As time went on, we realized that working from home (WFH) would become the workplace standard. Over two years later, I have only rarely set foot in our local headquarters. But the pace of work never slowed. I have still been booked solid in my typical 12 hours of back-to-back daily client calls, which morphed into all becoming nonstop video calls (never before have I been so casually dressed and yet so visible all day long). Yet there was a work–life balance that had eluded me in the past. The sanctioned bonus time from my commute-free existence meant I had more time to exercise and sleep. The proximity to my kids helped deepen my connection to their daily lives. Simple family dinners and game nights became a regular thing. As further evidence of our ability to work anytime, anyplace, and searches getting done more quickly, Russell Reynolds Associates had our biggest revenue year ever in 2021.

Equal Airtime

Videoconferencing tools like Zoom have now become an integral part of the way we work. The "future of work" has finally become our present. And the reality is that these tools can give a woman leader an advantage on multiple fronts. Broadly speaking, they are a means of visibility and networking that give access to all. While the picture of emerging technology and its effects on the workplace for women is nuanced, the clear upside is that they can be powerful weapons in the fight for parity. No longer does someone have to be judged negatively if she is stepping out of the office in the middle of the afternoon to take her child or elderly parent to a doctor's appointment, because it will be evident through her digital imprint that she's been just as productive as her colleagues, if not more, throughout the day.

As I mentioned at the beginning of this book, Zoom is a great corporate democratizer. It's much harder for one person to dominate the conversation in a Zoom meeting because each person's square is the same size. It is much easier to look at all your squares in one place than it is to crane your neck to look around a room to make sure everyone has had an opportunity to participate in the conversation. With everyone's faces before you, it's easier to observe their expressions to discern who might want to say something but is reluctant or shy until invited to speak. There is a whole new etiquette to videoconferencing that's more inclusive and makes us less at the mercy of the alpha personalities in the room.

"It's not just about who has the title, or who has inserted himself most," observed Elena Gomez, chief financial officer (CFO) of Toast, a cloud-based technology platform for restaurants.

Videoconferencing has also democratized access. It's much easier to grab five minutes of facetime with your boss or mentor, for example. Getting a meeting with a client used to require weeks of back and forth between administrative assistants to get lunch or coffee on the schedule. Often it would require flying to their city, taking time away from family and other work tasks. If you are a busy mom, logistically those dealmaking connections can be much harder to make.

"With Zoom it's just a quick call and you're in," said Elena.

But the result can be just as impactful, enabling these women to bring in more customers and show more results, furthering their careers and moving them faster along on the parity path without having to rack up all those airmiles.

Output Versus Input

Of course, the big question on the minds of leaders is productivity. Many companies still don't fully trust those who are off-site and unseen. They focus on input, concerned that individuals aren't plugged in nine to five, rather than the output that truly matters. But data-driven organizations that are carefully measuring output are beginning to realize that past notions of how a hard-working, go-getting employee behaves don't necessarily line up with the facts. Again, the assumption was that the mom who leaves early to pick up her child from school isn't getting the same results as the guy who is always in the office. The first to get in and the last to leave must definitionally be the best, right? Or not.

"When we look at the outputs, it forces us to reassess our ideas around bias more honestly," Christa told me. "People thought, Bob's doing a great job. He's getting in at 7 a.m. and leaving at 9 p.m. He's a real killer. But we never really knew what Bob was doing all day. He could have been sitting in his office watching Netflix. (Christa was speaking hypothetically, of course.)

Digital empowerment, smartly managed with measurable results, favors the quiet achievers. As Susan Cain so smartly observed in *Quiet*, her seminal book on the power of introverts, "There's zero correlation between being the best talker and having the best ideas."[4]

We might be attending a parent-teacher meeting at 4 p.m., but we've been powering through one client call after another since 7 a.m., and we'll be reading reports and whitepapers starting again at 7 p.m., once we've fed, bathed, and tucked in our kids, until 10 p.m. That level of input isn't visible to our colleagues or bosses, and not all of us are inclined to shout from the rooftops about it.

There are ways to track how many calls an employee made, how many engagements with potential customers, the duration of the engagements, and closure rates. What I do each day as a leadership advisor, for example, is highly measurable in terms of the revenue it generates for my firm. Although I might enjoy it, I don't need to schmooze in person or be seen at my desk to get the work done.

The Human Touch

For all its advantages, remote work obviously needs to be well-managed, and this is a new muscle that we are collectively building. Leaders can't afford to lose touch with the people behind the Zoom screens.

The possibility of being "on" and available 24/7 can easily lead to burnout, for example. Zoom fatigue is real, and leaders need to check in more often with individual team members to encourage healthy work habits. Encourage feedback and never assume that technology solves everything.

Being digitally connected is part of daily work life for Jennifer Goldfarb, co-founder of Ipsy, the iconic Silicon Valley-based online beauty company that was born out of the YouTube beauty movement. Like most companies during the pandemic, working remotely and relying on technology for connectivity became even more the case, to the point where the script flipped, and most interaction was through digital screens. But the shift prompted Jen to become more intentional about those in-person moments. When members of her team do enter the same physical space together, Jen tries to make it special, so it's not just another day in the office. Rather, it is an event with real purpose behind it – an office or conference that's designed to be memorable.

"It's almost like the digital is for the day to day and then we bring people together for collaboration, team building, rapport building, all of the stuff that used to come from everybody being immersed with each other five days a week," Jen told me. "Technology is great for getting things done efficiently, but maybe a totally digital world is less good for some of the softer but important aspects of building a company, such as blue-sky thinking, creativity, or building rapport with a young team."

For all that is possible in a virtual workplace setting, it's about balancing and managing it, and injecting more meaning into those in-person moments that we once took for granted.

Micro Moments

Toast's Elena Gomez is another leader who recognized the need to radically change the way we work. As a senior finance leader at companies including Visa, Charles Schwab, Salesforce, and Zendesk, she has a track record of implementing tools and making cultural adjustments to enhance quality of life and diversity among her team members. But it was at Zendesk, a global customer support software company, where she served as CFO during the first months of the pandemic, that she embraced tools like "Wellness Wednesdays" and "Recharge Fridays" to accommodate the work–life needs of her diverse team members.

Elena came to the realization that there was a need to build in some room to breathe when she caught a glimpse into the lives of her direct reports over Zoom.

Seeing moms with small children running around in the background, or moms having to nurse babies during a meeting, juggling it all on their own because they didn't have the resources for a babysitter, reminded Elena, whose own kids were a little older, that there was a whole other dimension to the lives of these individuals who were doing their best to show up in those uncertain times.

"We developed this thesis that if we don't give people a mental break, they're not going to be the best version of themselves at work. By offering them some flexibility at home with their partner, to take their child to the doctor or whatever their need was, they would be less tired or distracted."

Busy working moms loved the program, although it was meant for everyone, including men.[5] It had to be inclusive because, with everyone tethered to their technology beyond normal office hours, the prospect of Zoom burnout loomed large regardless of family status or demographics. Across 20 countries Zendesk implemented free digital mental health programs, mindfulness training, and coaching, as well as clinical support for those who needed it.

Zendesk has since mandated that all their employees take the second Friday of every month off to rest and recharge, so that no one feels singled out for choosing the timeout and "women don't feel it is focused on them," Elena explained. The result is a grateful and more engaged workforce. While Elena is no longer there, as a leader she's taken these insights with her to Toast, which has a less formal though no less intentional approach with the same principles, avoiding scheduling meetings on Friday, offering counseling, and being more liberal with their leave policy in recognition of the stress and isolation wrought by national and global events.

"In return you get happier, more engaged employees, potentially more loyalty, and that translates to better retention over time," Elena explained. "Think about how you feel when you come back from vacation. You have perspective and you feel reenergized."

Beyond policies and broad-based programs for wellness, Elena also makes a point of checking in with her people as individuals.

"As a leader, you've got to show empathy," she told me. "Acknowledge the difficult times and have those micro moments. *Hey, how's it going?* All those big programs don't replace the day-to-day interactions. Human kindness, especially in this environment, goes a long way. And when you're behind Zoom for so long, you have to be intentional about how to make connections with your colleagues. Even a 15-minute check-in can be incredibly impactful. It's likely a micro moment in a day but to the person you have connected with, the impact can be exponential."

"The fact that flexibility at work has been embraced is a beacon of hope," Elena told me. It's about everyone who works. If you're female, especially someone who is raising kids, even better. But it's a good thing that women don't feel it is isolated to their needs."

The rising tide lifts all boats, creating more room for diverse perspectives, experiences, and identities, which may ultimately lead us to the full democratization of corporate life. And women leaders are playing a huge part in enabling this change.

"If we can evolve that dramatically in two years, if we can change the norm after it's been the norm for over a hundred years, proving that this new way of working works for everyone, why can't we make this change to have more women run companies?" Elena asked.

We've seen a revolution in the workplace, but this is only the beginning. This new environment of flexibility, access, and empathy could become the launchpad that finally gets us to 50–50 at the highest levels. As "Sapient Leader" Elena well noted, "What we thought was impossible became possible right before our eyes."

Below the Zoom Line

Dame Vivian Hunt, Senior Partner Emeritus at McKinsey's London office and author of *The Power of Parity*, agrees. She found that these digital workplace tools, when well-managed, could free up time otherwise spent on routine or transactional tasks. For organizations operating on a hybrid model, that two or three days in the office should be quality time spent enriching relationships with our teams, expanding our networks, and investing in the professional development of ourselves and each other. Whatever we do with it, that time spent away from home needs to be valued at a premium.

"When I am staying out late or traveling for work it is a major priority for me to make that time away from my family even more effective and impactful," said Dame Vivian.

Making remote work *work* is a matter of checking in with the whole person. Dame Vivian is a fan of Zoom and the "powerful, thoughtful, and engaging content" she receives online when engaging with her peers. As an author, all the discussions I've had for this book have been on Zoom, Microsoft Teams, or Google Meet, and the conversations with the women leaders I have quoted on these pages have been so fascinating and enlightening that we often lost track of time and went well beyond our allotted time. These kinds of exchanges are made possible when you are working with a group of skilled and motivated individuals, whether they are colleagues or interview subjects. But it remains incumbent upon leaders to put in the effort and bring about those deeper conversations.

"We have to remember to swipe right and see everyone on our screens," said Dame Vivian, "Team leaders should be intentional online. We should manage hybrid working proactively to deliver inclusive and productive meetings."

"Lots of things happen below the Zoom line." Dame Vivian was reminded of this fact with a jolt when she learned that one of her direct reports was about to go on maternity leave. For months during the pandemic, her only contact with the woman had been via Zoom, from the neck up. Her facial features changed very little throughout those months, so Dame Vivian had no idea.

"Having had children myself, I can't imagine working with someone and them not knowing that I was pregnant."

As a senior leader, she blamed herself for the oversight.

"I must apologize to you for not knowing about what will probably be one of the most important thing to happen in your life," she said to the woman.

"Why?" the associate asked her. "I never told you."

"Yes, but in these last nine months I should have checked in and asked about your life beyond just, 'How are you?' – I should have been more curious," Dame Vivian explained to her. "It would surely have come out if I had made the effort to probe just a bit further in our conversations."

The associate had always been treated with the utmost professional respect. As she did with all her team members, Dame Vivian supported, coached, and mentored this expectant mother in ways that enabled her to excel at her job. She has high potential, with plenty of opportunities to develop within the firm. Yet if this colleague were to ever leave McKinsey, "it will be because she is in an environment where she doesn't feel seen and known, even by people who mean well and have good intentions," Dame Vivian explained.

So by all means, leverage technology for flexibility and inclusion. But never forget the human life that lives and breathes beyond those pixels. "You can become so 'efficient' that you aren't building real relationships. When this happens, you are short-changing yourself and your colleagues in the process."

Instead, use the precious time and freedom clawed back by this technology for "building soft skills, investing in relationships, and coaching, both giving and receiving it," Dame Vivian continued. Make all that extra bandwidth count.

Of course, it's not just Zoom that's rewriting the rules of the workplace (and leadership). We now have a whole slew of tech tools at our fingertips that, if harnessed effectively, could end up being a game changer for the visibility of women in the corporate world.

When Agnes Heftberger first relocated to Singapore with IBM in February 2022, many of the countries in her remit were still in lockdown. In her new role as general manager and technology leader of IBM ASEANZK, she had the monumental task of merging operations in nine fast-growing and strategically important markets across Australia, Southeast Asia, New Zealand, and Korea. Top of mind was how to create a new organization and community across such a diverse geography – not least because the pandemic was still forcing everyone to work remotely and in-person meetings were not happening.

Since the 1990s, IBM has invested in the infrastructure and tools to enable employees to work from anywhere. But being able to log in and see the faces of your colleagues and customers doesn't necessarily solve the problem of managing projects that require true collaboration, alignment, creativity, and innovation.

Agnes was looking for feedback on strategic topics like market opportunities, cultural transformation, and collaboration, and knew that she had to find a way to enable individuals who had never been in the same room together to share ideas and brainstorm – even if they're not sitting around the same table with a whiteboard, coffee, and takeout sandwiches. How could she make it work without that human chemistry of being face to face?

The answer was to use IBM's companywide messaging platform for a four-day-long "storm" that gathered feedback across nine countries and eight product groups. Through this system, IBMers could work from different locations in a way that was asynchronistic, catching up in their own time, asking questions and sharing updates without having to coordinate their schedules.

But Agnes took it a step further. Her leadership teams started having other real-time remote brainstorming sessions.

"We asked ourselves, 'What are the most burning issues in terms of establishing this new market?" Agnes recalled.

They distilled these concerns into four themes, then every day on a company-wide messaging platform, the leadership team solicited 12,000 items of feedback from associates on specific questions. People could jump on various threads to discuss and exchange ideas, then vote on which solution they thought best.

"It gave us a way to innovate," Agnes explained. "It enabled us to collaborate across cultural differences, different job roles, and different parts of the organizations in remote ways."

The Data Advantage

Of course, there is a whole menu of team collaboration tools now available for remote work, including cloud storage, file-sharing, instant messaging, digital whiteboards, and document synchronization. Some may be more appropriate than others depending on the size of your organization, the composition of your teams, and the nature of your industry.

For a woman competing for those top positions yet not completely comfortable declaring her accomplishments, the evidence is also right there in the data. These tools can get her the credit she deserves for the ideas she's put forth in a Slack message, for example, because she is tagged on that message no matter how many conversation threads get woven around it in companywide discourse. This digital trail makes it difficult for co-workers to claim another person's ideas as their own.

Virtual workplace technology can also give a female employee access to invitation-only women's networks and affinity groups where she can talk openly about discrimination, unfair compensation practices, and other challenges, while receiving moral support and suggestions for solutions from her Slack comrades. In short, these platforms can be galvanizing, spurring women into action who might otherwise have kept silent or confided only in a trusted friend.[6]

Even more openly, in companywide Slack chats, women have become more emboldened to speak up. In more traditional collaborative settings that hasn't always been the case. Research by Princeton and Brigham Young Universities in 2012 found that men typically take up 75% of the conversation in meetings where there is a mixed populations around the table.[7]

Of course, the digital empowerment revolution applies to some industries more than others. A November 2020 McKinsey[8] study found that the finance and insurance industries have the highest potential for remote work, with workers reporting they have the ability to spend 75% of their time working remotely without a loss of productivity. There are many industries in which operations can't be carried out from home, including construction, film production, transportation, and healthcare, but the study finds that most exist on a "spectrum of flexibility." The research suggests that there is some economic disparity between those who can take advantage of remote work and those who cannot. The potential for remote work is most concentrated for highly skilled and highly educated workers in the most developed economies. But for women managers, professionals, and executives at least, the normalization of remote work in industries where it is possible is undoubtedly a win.

What was initially regarded as just a means of getting through to the other side of the lockdowns has, in many respects, led to a new and, in my opinion, better standard for how we interact in the workplace setting. And, with the right digital infrastructure, organizations can bring even more flexibility into the workplace. These solutions would, in turn, include women and other underrepresented groups who could get onto a faster leadership track when they're enabled and empowered to show up for their working lives in more nontraditional, remote ways.

As Christa Quarles, the CEO of Alludo introduced in the first pages of this book, so aptly put it, "Why would anyone with a blank sheet of paper want to create the 2019 version of an office?"

* * *

Your Path to the Top Checklist

Embrace the flexibility and hybrid work models brought about by the pandemic lockdowns. This will empower not just you personally as a woman leader managing work–life balance, but also for your teams. If companies adhere to old norms, they are going to miss the boat on the top diverse talent in the market.

Find where you sit on the spectrum of flexibility. Leverage digital solutions to give back much-needed bandwidth to leaders, enabling them to focus on what matters most.

It is possible to achieve more remotely than you think. When used correctly, digital software and apps can democratize data, empowering everyone with the information they need to contribute and to be recognized for their output.

Creativity doesn't have to be synchronized. Programs like Slack enable collaboration across cultural differences, time zones, different job roles, and various parts of the organization in ways that can be both inclusive and seamless.

Rebuild the culture in a remote-hybrid world. Invest in the technology and digital services that enhance the remote and hybrid work experience. Go beyond basic videoconferencing to enable a sense of engagement and well-being outside the four walls of the office.

Democratize airtime via new Zoom etiquette. With everyone's face before you, it's easier to observe their expressions and discern who might want to say something but is reluctant or shy until invited to speak. Use videoconferencing to be more inclusive.

Measure output, not input. Data-driven organizations that are carefully measuring output are beginning to realize that past notions of how a hard-working, go-getting employee behaves don't necessarily line up with the facts. It is less about who shows up at the office for 12 hours in person and more about how many calls were made, how many engagements with potential customers, the duration of the engagements, closure rates, and so on. It is often the quiet achievers who are getting it done.

Don't forget the human beyond the Zoom box. Remote work needs to be well-managed. Leaders can't afford to lose touch with the individual behind the digital screen.

PART TWO

Leaps and Upward Bounds

CHAPTER 4

Seen and Heard

It took me quite a long time to develop a voice, and now that I have it, I am not going to be silent.

—Madeleine K. Albright

I t was perfectly galling. Over the three and a half years Julia Gillard, the 27th prime minister of Australia, had been in office, she'd been subjected to a stream of sexist insults. The commentary about the country's first woman to serve as deputy prime minister and prime minister was savage and, often, obscene. She had delivered nation-changing policies in education, sustainability, and healthcare, and made strides towards improving the country's mental health programs. She also led Australia through one of the worst economic crises in its history. Yet it seemed all the local opposition politicians and media pundits cared about were the size of her breasts, the tone of her voice, and the fit of her pantsuits.

So, when the leader of the opposition party, Tony Abbott, brought forward a motion in 2012 to have the Speaker of the House of Representatives removed after it was revealed he'd sent some misogynistic texts, suggesting that it was a reflection on Ms. Gillard herself, she was compelled to speak out. "I will not be lectured about sexism and misogyny by this man. I will not," she said. "And the government will not be lectured about sexism and misogyny by this man. Not now, not ever."

Ms. Gillard went on to list some of the egregious comments and actions made by Abbott. Like the fact that he proudly stood next to a placard that read "Ditch the Witch" in reference to her. Like the occasion he told an interviewer, in response to the suggestion that women were underrepresented in Australian institutions, "If it's true. . .that men have more power generally speaking than women, is that a bad thing?"

"This is the man from whom we're supposed to take lectures about sexism?" asked Ms. Gillard, rhetorically of course.

Righteous Indignation

The passion and indignance in Ms. Gillard's voice animated her words as she skillfully took this man down with his own outrageous and hateful statements. She was succinct, devastatingly to the point, and unwavering in her delivery. Ms. Gillard was powered by righteous anger because they weren't just insults directed at her; they were demeaning and insulting to *all* women.

"I was also very offended on behalf of the women of Australia when in the course of this carbon pricing campaign, the Leader of the Opposition said, 'What the housewives of Australia need to understand as they do the ironing. . .'" Ms. Gillard said. "Thank you for that painting of women's roles in modern Australia."

The personal attacks leading up to what has since become known as the "Misogyny Speech" had, until then, been endured with "a bitten lip." The prime minister had been trying to rise above, not wanting the petty distractions to throw her off course as she focused her attention on leading the country. But enough was enough.

"The Leader of the Opposition says that people who hold sexist views and who are misogynists are not appropriate for high office. Well, I hope the Leader of the Opposition has got a piece of paper and he is writing out his resignation. Because if he wants to know what misogyny looks like in modern Australia, he doesn't need a motion in the House of Representatives, he needs a mirror. That's what he needs."

When the former world leader spoke with my colleagues a decade later in 2022, on our *Redefiners* podcast,[1] she shared what was going through her mind and heart in the moments leading up to that career-defining speech, which broke records as the most watched political event in Australian media history, with millions of views on YouTube.

"I didn't know I was going to make that speech, and I didn't prepare for it at all," she said.

She knew the subject of sexism might come up during the ritual of Parliament's "rough and tumble" question time because of the recent unmasking of her Speaker's inappropriate tweets. But she had not expected Abbott to go straight there. So she started furiously scribbling notes. All at once the unfairness of years of double standards of Abbott, his party, and the entire political system hit her. Would a man have been described as unfit to lead because he was unmarried and childless?

It all erupted, and in that moment Ms. Gillard's authentic voice rang out so loud she made history. She never imagined that 10 years later people would still be talking about it, but she is grateful that it happened. While she had always considered herself to be a feminist, this was the speech that crystallized her mission to bring about gender equality. Today she is the inaugural chair of the Global Institute of Women's Leadership at King's College London, and holds board seats on a host of business and philanthropic organizations, including the Global Partnership for Education, which works to ensure every child receives a quality school education.

"I was of that generation of women in my political party that fought for more women in Parliament through an affirmative action rule. When we were in government, obviously we were trying to do the right thing on women's equality. But the speech, I guess, is the moment that that got defined globally. So my recognition now around those causes – women in leadership, feminism, gender equality – exploded because of it. And that's given me all sorts of opportunities I possibly wouldn't have had without it."

Drowned Out

Ms. Gillard is an especially high-profile example of what can unfold when you find your voice. It just so happened that hers broke through on the global stage. For many women leaders it can be a struggle to get seen and heard. Often, we are the only ones at the table, in the boardroom, or speaking at a conference. The power of our voices gets muffled as we are talked over, mansplained, dismissed, or ignored. Our opinions are often met with skepticism while our male colleagues' views are received with credibility and respect. Assumptions about what leadership looks like, and how we should look, sound, or carry ourselves can undermine our self-confidence. Without role models – a way to see it and be it – it can often take us a few extra beats to come into our own.

It's no different whether we are talking about political institutions, medical schools, or global corporations. The false and outdated perceptions that persist at the leadership level were so glaring to Ms. Gillard that she co-authored a book with Dr. Ngozi Okonjo-Iweala, director general of the World Trade Organization. Titled *Women in Leadership: Real Lives, Real Lessons,* the book is a call to action. Women hold less than 10% of CEO seats in the largest 100 companies in the S&P 500, and this lack of access to power boils down to some deeply ingrained, patriarchal mindsets.

As Ms. Gillard explained, "We've got to get away from fixing women, telling women to do things differently, and start fixing structures and eradicating stereotypes. All the big power structures in our societies have developed over time and they've been based on the rhythm of men's lives. And we are pretty slow about the task of adapting them to women's lives."

After living under this system for centuries, it's hard to break free of this way of thinking. To varying degrees, we've all been conditioned.

"Because we've grown up in a gendered environment, we all have gendered stereotypes in the back of our brain, which means that we tend to correlate men and leadership and we don't do the same for women," Ms. Gillard observed.

Guilty

> *Obviously, I am huge proponent of women's leadership, but even I have been guilty of unconscious bias. Last year, upon boarding a plane, I was greeted by a woman I assumed to be a flight attendant. She was wearing the airline uniform after all. But 30 minutes later, after takeoff, I heard an announcement from "First Officer Anderson" welcoming all of us passengers onto her flight. It was only then I realized that the woman I saw was actually the pilot. Shame on me for making such a sexist assumption, but I promise you that I'll never make that mistake again!*

Flexing Leadership Muscles

When I first started working as an associate at RRA 20 years ago, one of the first skill sets that I had to master was writing compelling and thorough candidate letters to present to our clients in advance of in-person interviews. These letters are both historical summaries of a person's career, as well as our written evaluation of the candidate's strengths and weaknesses against the position specification, both in terms of their experiences to date and their behavioral competencies for the job. At the time, I was told that a now-retired partner in my firm, who happened to live in the Midwest, wrote the best "CLs" (as we internally refer to them), and that I should try to emulate his when writing mine.

When I dutifully pulled several from our database to review, I noticed that one of the introductions read, "He walks in from Central Casting. Standing confidently six feet, three inches tall with a thick head of salt and pepper hair and piercing blue eyes, John has been married to his college sweetheart Mary for 25 years."

Wait. . .what?!

Thank goodness much has changed since then. Through our more recent work, we now know that the most successful CEOs, COOs, CMOs, CFOs, and other senior executives look nothing like that rather embarrassing, sexist typecasting.

Today's most successful leaders cannot be pigeonholed. RRA's research shows the best executives are able to flex their approach, bringing different skills to the fore, depending on the specific situation they face. They embody both "loud" and "quiet" competencies. They show both rational and emotional intelligence. And they are able to demonstrate contradictory, sometimes anachronistic ways of showing up, almost simultaneously.

It is this paradoxical expression of personality (and the resulting agility) that sets great leaders apart. These traits are not at odds with each other; they happily coexist. And they give leaders the much-needed dexterity to navigate an uncertain and fast-moving world. As each new situation arises, these top executives understand exactly which behaviors they need to draw upon to find a way forward. Through our empirically validated research, we found the most effective C-suite leaders typically "span" four dualities:

- **Disruptive and pragmatic.** Great leaders know when to disrupt the status quo with innovation, and when to be pragmatic about focus, priorities, and the pace of transformation.

- **Risk-taking and reluctant.** Great leaders know when to take calculated risks and be opportunistic, and when to show vigilance before steering the organization off a cliff.

- **Heroic and vulnerable.** Great leaders are heroic, but they are also vulnerable, knowing how to ensure that perseverance and grit don't turn into self-delusions. They take feedback and external data to heart and make continuous improvements to themselves and their organizations.

- **Galvanizing and connecting.** Great leaders galvanize support with energy and inspiration, but they also know when to take a step back, share credit, and promote the success of others. They can connect the organization to become something stronger and greater than themselves and the cult of their own personality.

Of course, it can be hard to find your voice when you've been told for so long to hide certain personality traits if you want to succeed. We've all been conditioned at some points of our lives – directly or indirectly – to act more like a man if we want to get ahead. But what RRA's leadership model makes clear is that great leadership is nuanced. And that gives room for different leaders to come forward from the ones we might have seen in the past. It allows us to avoid cookie-cutter approaches to leadership and to be much more accepting of the full gamut of personality. When you realize this, it becomes a lot easier to be your whole, authentic self at work, rather than trying to emulate an almost caricatured leadership style from days of old (yet still widely perpetuated in popular culture).

So what does this new face of leadership look like? Probably not the John Hamm lookalike from Central Casting. But it may resemble Julie Greenwald, chairwoman and CEO of Atlantic Records Group and a self-described "Jewish mom" in her leadership style. She is equal parts grit, determination, and compassion. In a business that faces the constant churn of disruption, Julie and the record label she runs would be obsolete if she wasn't as demanding of herself as she is of others – hard-driving, unaccepting of excuses (or as she puts it, "BS"), and even a little cantankerous at times:

"I am tough as nails," Julie told me. "I'm definitely one of the scariest people who walks the halls. But I have to be, because this is not an industry of widgets. The business keeps changing underneath our feet, like building something on quicksand. This is an industry of art and music, and technology is changing how our consumers discover and pay for our music every day, which is how we support and pay for our artists. Which is why I need to show strength and make sure we are living up to our obligation to take care of them. I've got to guide them to safety."

At the same time, Julie knows how to turn down the volume on that commanding voice of hers.

"There also has to be real humanity in the workplace," said Julie. "People need to be able to feel like they can hug you and be open about their shitty day or share what's going on at home. I need to create a space where people can be vulnerable with me and express their concerns, personally and professionally."

"You've got to be tough, but you also have to be a human if you're going to motivate others. You want your teams to be inspired."

Julie perfectly models this ability to flex as she intuits what's going on with her team and what needs to happen for their well-being and the health of her business. Obviously, this balance of ingredients looks different depending on the individual and the right recipe of the industry you are in. Ultimately, every organization will have its own requirements for what people need from their senior executives, now and in the future. But from our work with forward-thinking companies around the world, we know that assessing whether a leader possesses the agility to flex between these four seemingly paradoxical traits can be a strong indicator of whether they will thrive in the C-suite.

But I...

This new and proven model for successful leadership is precisely why we need to develop a more heightened awareness of ingrained biases, and to be more proactive about eradicating those stereotypes so that they don't distort the way decisions are made. Mary Ann Sieghart, the author of *The Authority Gap* and whom I introduced in Chapter 1, cites countless examples of women's voices being disregarded based on gender stereotyping.

"The authority gap is the extent to which we're still much more prepared to accord authority to men than to women," she explained in our *Redefiners* podcast. "And when I say authority, I mean both in terms of expertise and in terms of power and leadership. The result is all sorts of behaviors, which is incredibly frustrating for women, such as being underestimated, undermined, interrupted, or talked over, having their expertise disproportionately challenged, finding it much harder to influence a group, and having their power or authority resisted."

One landmark study that proves her case involves the US Supreme Court from 2017,[2] when women made up a third of all justices, which found the women on the Bench suffered two-thirds of all interruptions. In other words, they were four times more likely to be interrupted than their male counterparts, 96% of the time by men.

The author and journalist also referenced the age-old "but I just said that" phenomenon, when a woman makes a point in a meeting, only to be ignored and, ten minutes later, a man says the exact same thing, and "it gets treated like the Second Coming."

"This often happens," notes Ms. Sieghart. "And we tend to beat ourselves up about it. And we think, 'Oh, maybe I wasn't confident enough, or maybe I wasn't articulate or eloquent enough.' No, you were probably just too female."

As if further evidence of this fact is needed, Ms. Sieghart points to the example of Joan Roughgarden, an evolutionary biologist who transitioned from male to female. When she was living as a man he kept getting promoted, his salary kept going up, he was invited to sit on important committees, and his work was taken seriously. When she started living as a woman, she found no one would listen to her until a male colleague confirmed what she said. She was struck by how many times she would present an argument, only to be told, "You obviously haven't read the literature" – something that never happened to her as a man.

"Her conclusion was that men are assumed to be competent until they prove otherwise. Women are assumed to be incompetent until they prove otherwise," said Ms. Sieghart.

Over the years, many people have put the responsibility to fix this problem on women, advising us to hone our meeting and vocal skills to get ourselves heard. But the problem does not lie with women. The problem is in how women's voices and leadership are received. The solution is to trust in our own voices and persist.

It's why this new era requires a different kind of roadmap for leadership development, in which women can find their own voices, and be heard with respect. And it should no longer be necessary for women to emulate stereotypic male behaviors to get ahead. We can draw upon our own effective ways of being to benefit our teams, our families, and the world. In fact, it's time to celebrate and embrace qualities like vulnerability, authenticity, and compassion. We need to permit ourselves to make mistakes and refuse to be typecast.

And ditch that perfectionism! For all her moxie, Atlantic Records Group's Julie Greenwald recalls struggling to accept higher job titles. She fell into that trap of thinking she had to meet a long checklist of qualifications and experience to earn a title that, frankly, any man much less qualified wouldn't hesitate to jump at. She recalled the day more than 20 years ago when her boss, Lyor Cohen, called her into his office and told her he would be making her president of Island Records, the label they both worked for at the time.

"Do you think I'm ready?" Julie asked him.

"You've been running the company this whole time," he told her. "Of course you're ready!"

Nail Power

Marianne Bergmann Røren, CEO of the Norwegian road and highway construction giant Mesta, whom we met in Chapter 1, could not have found herself in a more male-dominated business. When she joined, there wasn't a single woman on the management team. Having come from the worlds of law and banking,

Marianne was accustomed to an environment where "everyone fit the same profile, so to speak." She wasn't okay with the lack of diversity, and she had hoped for a change in those dynamics with each career move. Her extreme competence and professionalism kept propelling her higher at each organization, until she ended up as a top executive in Danske Bank.

From that high finance corporate role to being at the helm of a company that builds roads, creates bridges, and carves tunnels into mountains, I just had to ask her, "Was it hard to be yourself in those testosterone-driven environments?"

At first, it was. But Marianne refused to be anything but her authentic, feminine self. Her coiffed blonde hair and nails (painted cherry red on our Zoom call) were impeccable. She accessorized, and wore flowery dresses and heels. She told me that her PR team would love her to look more the part of a gritty road engineer when she's interviewed by the media, but she refuses.

"Unless it's for safety reasons and I am on a construction site, I see no reason why I should have to wear a hard hat or overalls," she told me. "That's not who I am, and it doesn't have to be."

It's not that Marianne hasn't had to deal with plenty of sexism on the job. She's been told to "take it like a man" and calmly but wittily responded, "Well, that's a little bit difficult, because I am a woman." When she was more junior in her career, in one of her first meetings with senior partners at her law firm, she'd spent days preparing her presentation, only to have one of the 20 men at the table ask her as she began her presentation, "How old are you, really?" It threw her off her whole speech. But, over the years, she taught herself to focus on what really matters to the business.

The solid foundation of an upbringing with two sisters and a father who repeatedly reminded them that they could do anything stayed with her and helped her stay focused on what mattered. Besides, "I've found it is too exhausting to internalize everything," Marianne shared with me. While it is important to hold your ground or call someone out for behavior that crosses the line, "You can't dwell too much on the small stuff. You need to go a little bit like this," she said, symbolically motioning to flick something off her shoulder. So when members of her team proposed a bonding weekend of hunting, she said, "No thanks." She also politely declined the suggestion that they all stay at a lodge with "a great hot tub," although she was quick to point out the men meant nothing untoward about it. "But no, I am not going to get in there with you guys and drink beers," she told them, with a chuckle.

Marianne's own unique blend of grace and humor has helped her to stand out as a great leader among her peers. Her unflappable professionalism got her noticed and helped her to "float up."

But it has long been her goal *not* to be the only one, and her ascent to CEO at Mesta has made her more determined to create an environment where other women feel comfortable letting their voices be seen and heard. In Chapter 1, I described how Marianne made bold moves to bring 50–50 parity to Mesta's leadership team, from a total of zero. But she doesn't stop there:

"When you create diversity, you need to also make it work by creating a place and space for that diversity to thrive."

She intentionally builds an open and trust-based environment where people feel that their diverse points of view will be welcomed. She makes it clear that women can show up as themselves, and she models that behavior. She leaves her door open for anyone to walk in and share a concern or opinion. She makes sure no one feels like they have to have a beer with the boys after work to fit in. It is about taking advantage of the diversity once it exists, "where women can not only get the job and participate, but actually thrive, be happy, and feel motivated."

Leaving Loud

Sarah Mensah, vice president and general manager, North America, at Nike Inc., is a transformational leader for many reasons. But one of my favorite stories she shared with me was how she leaves the office when she's going to pick up her son from a soccer game, or really anything to do with her family. She "leaves loud" and makes a point of announcing to the people in the room where she's going, why, and that she'll be available on her cell phone if they need her. It's her way of letting everyone know it's okay to have a life outside of work, and that people can bring their authentic selves to work. That is exactly the kind of role modeling women need to see to feel supported and empowered. By using her voice, she is giving voice.

See It to Be It

Again, finding your voice, that inner confidence to make yourself heard, can come from within, when your own character and upbringing breaks through the external noise of assumptions and stereotyping, as it did in Marianne's case. A woman can be the only one and have an impact. But there's greater power in numbers. Elena Gomez, whom you first met in Chapter 3, was taken aback on her second day at Zendesk, when a random employee walked up to her and said, "You cannot imagine how happy we are that you are here!"

Apparently, a memo had circulated around the company with Elena's bio a week before she joined, so when she walked in she felt a like a minor celebrity. She tried to make some smalltalk with this associate, asking her about her role in the company and a little about her life, but her new colleague continued to gush, "'For so long we have been wanting to look up and see someone like you,' she said. 'It's amazing to see a woman *and* a person of color in your role at the leadership level. It gives us hope.' It was at that moment I realized what was possible by being in this role. I was the example, the one who could create an impact."

Zendesk built on that impact, bringing in a chief people officer who was also a woman of color, "so when you start seeing that you have a lot more hope." But the inclusive culture that allows women to be heard also requires deliberate steps and attention to detail. It's about reading a room and noticing each person.

"It's not just about getting people in the seat, because it's one thing to get them into a meeting, and it's another to let them share their voice in the meeting."

Seeing diversity in action at meetings takes women like Elena, with their already established voices, as well as men, going around the room or the table and directly inviting them to speak. One time, Elena noticed a woman seated with her at the boardroom table, and she could tell from the woman's body language that she had something to contribute. But the woman, who held a more junior title like director, stayed quiet, holding herself back because she was intimidated by the more senior and mostly male executives in the room. Elena recognized the signs because she'd lived that experience at a previous organization, where there would be six men in the room to two women, including herself. It was hard enough to express herself to a senior executive from a more junior position, but the way the men carried themselves, that body language of confidence and the palpable sense that they belonged amplified this sense of power imbalance.

"I would say to her, 'Jenna, what do you think?' to draw her out. I would hope that more women in my position would do that for each other, but it really takes the entire management team to make that cultural shift of including everyone," Elena told me.

A Fine Mess

Before you can use your voice to call on the voices of others, you need to dig deep to discover what works for you, then give yourself permission to be authentic, free of the pressure to be perfect that so many of us put on ourselves. We're all human, with self-doubt, foibles, private pains, passions, dreams, and hopes. While I am not suggesting that we should let it all hang out, we need to acknowledge that everyone's life gets a little messy sometimes, and that's okay. As leaders, it doesn't serve us to keep a hard line between our public and private selves. The more we integrate our occasionally chaotic humanity into our interactions with those who report to us, the more relatable and accessible we become as leaders and role models for others.

Recall Dame Vivian Hunt from Chapter 3, a Senior Partner Emeritus at McKinsey's London office whose career trajectory has been so outstanding that, in 2018, she was appointed by Queen Elizabeth II to be Dame Commander of the Order of the British Empire for services to the economy and women in business – a rare honor for someone American-born and raised. The list of Dame Vivian's accomplishments as a leader, thinker, and mentor is impressive and extensive. She sits on boards and councils ranging from the Confederation of British Industry, the Mayor of London's Business Advisory Council, Harvard University, The British Museum and The Southbank Centre where she is a trustee. She is also the chair of Teach First, the UK's leading educational charity, of which His Majesty King Charles III is the Patron, and the founding Chair of the Black Equity Organisation (BEO), the UK's first national Black civil rights organization. The *Financial Times* also identified Dame Vivian, who holds British citizenship, as one of the "European Women to Watch" and one of the 30 most influential people in London.[3] And yet, she told me, "I came to the UK as a nearly six-foot-tall Black American woman looking to build a career in healthcare." Today, she is the Chief Innovation Officer at UnitedHealth Group.

She said, "I never thought that I was anyone's idea of what success can look like." Yet knowing this was freeing for Dame Vivian in a way. But it was a journey to get there. Dame Vivian shared how, when she first started at McKinsey, she cultivated a certain persona. Three years in at the firm, during her early leadership training when she was managing her first team, Dame Vivian experienced her first structured, 360-degree review. It was overwhelmingly positive. Clients and colleagues loved her. She was described as "analytic, extremely work-oriented, 100% reliable." She was also characterized as "buttoned up" and not particularly personable or warm, but "could really be trusted to get the work done."

For better or worse, that was exactly what Dame Vivian intended to project. During that initial phase of her career, she was being intentional about developing her technical skills and exceeding professional expectations as a new associate and manager. Yet she was wearing a mask.

"You have your posture towards your clients, your posture within the firm, and your posture to your team," she told me. "The people doing the review were parroting back exactly what I was putting out there. But it wasn't me."

Of course, finding and recognizing who that person is, is not necessarily like flipping a switch, especially when you are younger. Dame Vivian recommends seeking out coaches, advisors, even peers at work for feedback. Some of us wait to reach a certain benchmark, like a promotion, then lose a little of ourselves along the way, but it's worth the investment to restore and develop your authentic voice. Building that self-confidence in the early phase of your career can also come from role models – "from real life, not social media," Dame Vivian cautions.

"It's a little bit like knowing what looks good on you in terms of fashion. Don't try to look like somebody else or embrace some artificial, distorted image. Find someone whose style you admire and has your body shape, then pick and choose from the choices they are making."

Shop around for those – women or men – whose careers and leadership style you admire. When you're younger, it is understandable that you won't necessarily have your own life experience and extensive network of relationships to feel fully confident.

"It's important not to be too hard on individuals when they are at that point of uncertainty," Dame Vivian observed.

The patina of authenticity and self-awareness comes with time, so "fake it 'til you make it" as you absorb the history and learn the lessons of worthy role models, suggests Dame Vivian. And read. Dame Vivian has always devoured biographies of historical figures she admires, such as Nelson Mandela. But it's not necessarily their noble accomplishments that fascinate her. It's the stories behind the story – their all too human struggles. The fact that Mandela was divorced and estranged from his children, who learned more about their father from press stories than as a present dad, taught her that "true service and activism at a global scale requires sacrifice."

Unlocked

Finally, developing that strong, confident voice isn't just about being heard. We must be willing to hear and receive the insights of others, as long as they are coming from a place of constructive feedback. Reading that holistic, 360-review made Dame Vivian realize that, although the masks were working in terms of what she was trying to accomplish, she could be so much more. Dame Vivian was shielding parts of her bold self – a wicked sense of humor, her Christian faith (her father was a pastor), and her personal and family life – that could shine through organically without causing anyone to think less of her. In fact, just the opposite because, although Dame Vivian was succeeding with her masks, "there was one complication: it was exhausting."

Work felt like an endless performance, in which she was constantly being evaluated. Of course, to some degree she was, as we all are. But that didn't mean she needed to be quite so guarded.

"Carrying all these masks around just got to be too much."

Dame Vivian immediately decided to put them down. Though effective, the stress of maintaining multiple facades would not have been sustainable as she took on more responsibilities and ascended on the partner path. She had already proven she could deliver, so she decided her clients could accept her just as she was, individual quirks and all. Rather than "pre-secure how I was going to be interpreted," she let go. Then something surprising happened. The newfound ease of her interactions with others, which Dame Vivian thought was noticeable only to herself, was palpable on every level. Her emails took on a friendlier, more intimate tone. She laughed more, allowing her self-deprecating wit to shine through. Looking at before-and-after pictures, she could see a more relaxed expression on her face and in her body language.

"That was a big unlock moment for me," Dame Vivian said.

Around the same time, her role had shifted. She relocated overseas, took on the management of a sizeable team, and was entrusted with the responsibility of building a new practice within the firm. Her casual approach fit well with this more entrepreneurial role. It also strengthened the bond with her direct reports.

"It's especially liberating to have a manager or colleague who is just herself, because it frees you to say, 'Okay, if she can bring her whole self to work, then maybe I can too.'"

Finding her authentic voice was "a gift to myself" that kept on giving.

* * *

Your Path to the Top Checklist

It's not women who need to change. We've got to get away from fixing women and start changing structures and eradicating stereotypes. All the big power structures have been based on the rhythm of men's lives and it's time to adapt them to women's lives.

Acknowledge biases. We need to be more proactive about eradicating stereotypes so that they don't distort the way decisions are made. Assumptions about male expertise and authority result in women being underestimated, undermined, interrupted, or talked over, having their knowledge disproportionately challenged. Let's at least recognize that this is happening.

Trust in your own voice. We are sitting at the table because it's where we belong, so the onus is not on us to change how we communicate. The problem lies not in our delivery, but in how our listeners are failing to receive. The solution is to trust in our own voices and persist.

Don't internalize the small stuff. Some men may say stupid, insensitive things. But focusing on it too much is exhausting, so brush it off. Of course, if someone crosses the line, call it out and hold your ground. But don't dwell if it doesn't serve you.

Do you. It is no longer necessary to suppress certain traits. In fact, it's time to celebrate and embrace qualities like vulnerability, authenticity, and compassion. Talk about your life and share what's going on with your kids and family. Wear as much pink as you want to. You need to dig deep to discover what works for you, then give yourself permission to be authentic. Again, it's about bringing your whole self into the workplace.

Ditch perfectionism. We need to permit ourselves to make mistakes, free of the pressure to be perfect that so many of us put on ourselves. We're all human, with self-doubt, foibles, private pains, passions, dreams and hopes. Everyone's life gets a little messy sometimes and that's okay.

Integrate different facets of your life. As compassionate leaders, it doesn't serve us to keep a hard line between our public and private selves. The more we integrate our occasionally chaotic humanity into our interactions with those who report to us, the more relatable and accessible we become as leaders and role models for others.

Find role models. From real life, books, colleagues, peers, and mentors. When you are younger you may still be finding your voice, so "fake it 'til you make it" and look around to emulate the traits and strategies of those you admire most.

Hear what they're saying. Seek out coaches for a sense of how you are coming across. Developing your own voice isn't just about being heard. We must be willing to hear and receive the insights of others when they come from the right place in terms of career development and mentorship.

CHAPTER 5

The Art of the Ask

A woman's best protection is a little money of her own.
—Clare Boothe Luce

In early 2020, I was doing a search for a CFO position at a Fortune 50 industrial company headquartered in the Midwest. I had the perfect candidate, and the client was thrilled. But before the deal could be finalized, we needed salary comparisons. How much were people in similar positions, at the same executive level, in that particular industry, and in that particular region, being paid? I had my team pull together compensation benchmarks. When I looked at the spreadsheet, I was flabbergasted. Women CFOs were making 30% less than men.

This can't be right, I said to myself. We reran the data with a larger sample, looking at all Midwestern manufacturing companies with revenues of at least $10 billion. Still about a 30% differential. Then I broke down the numbers, slicing and dicing them at least a dozen different ways. Was the difference attributable to some having a CPA or audit background versus more Wall Street experience? Were the women less experienced? Younger? Were the companies underperforming, or did they have a lower PE ratio? Statistically, I could find no correlated data that made sense. In that particular industry, which encompassed 50 or more companies, the pay gap was ubiquitously present across the board.

I was so shocked and appalled that I considered going to the media with an exposé. Instead, I decided to use this data as a point of instruction to my clients, drawing their attention to the discrepancy and suggesting that this lack of financial parity did not serve these companies well. Imagine if the talent they are trying to hire should find out?

Most employers quickly grasp my point, especially in this era of external and internal pressure to meet environmental, social, and governance goals (ESG), not least among them diversity, equity, and inclusion (DE&I). Increasingly, legislation is requiring corporations to be more transparent about salary bands. And in some jurisdictions, companies are prohibited from asking job candidates about their previous pay packages – a disclosure that has been disadvantageous to women in the past since many are coming off lower baseline salaries. These new norms and regulations should help level the playing field. But we're not there yet.

The reasons for the lack of parity in compensation are complex and multifactorial. It's not just that companies are intentionally setting out to lowball the women they hire, although that does happen. The reasons are also cultural and historical. Many women recoil at the thought of having to ask for a pay increase.

According to an April 2021 survey by Glassdoor, a job search and employer review website, 73% of women said they have not asked for a raise during the pandemic, compared with 58% of men, while less than half of women planned to ask for a raise, bonus, or cost-of-living increase over the next year.[1]

"This trend is a continuation of what we were seeing before the pandemic," said Glassdoor career expert Alison Sullivan. "In a pandemic, an uncertain economy or job market leads to [women] putting off pay conversations because they don't want to rock the boat."[2]

While some men seem to have no problem bellying up and demanding promotions and raises, many women struggle with these conversations, often because we focus more on where our skill sets are lacking than on what our strengths are.

Historically, companies have gotten away with gendered pay discrepancy because financial literacy has not been taught early enough in the lives of girls and young women. So not only are some women less comfortable with these conversations than most men, but we haven't typically prioritized remuneration in terms of our career choices. We tend to opt for lower-paid specialties, for example, choosing to be pediatricians over orthopedic surgeons, for example. We're often at a lower baseline from the beginning of our career trajectory. With each promotion, review, or job change, the chasm gets wider and wider, to the point where it becomes next to impossible to catch up with our male counterparts.

Your Legacy

We need to be more strategic about women's financial well-being. Each new promotion comes not only with new roles and responsibilities, but a new floor of salary, bonuses, and equity that we need to reach and surpass. Failure to master this aspect of the path to parity puts us behind not just in terms of equity, but dignity, respect, and self-worth. We owe it to ourselves. We also owe it to those who come after us. This is about so much more than building a quality life for ourselves. It's about building a legacy.

"Asking for what I was worth and pushing for equality was not about buying another car or material item; it was so my kids, and *their* kids, could go to college debt-free," Titi Cole, CEO of Legacy Franchises at Citigroup, told me.

The Nigerian-American financial executive grew up in a family of academics and high achievers. Education was everything. After Titi left Nigeria to pursue an MBA at Northwestern University's Kellogg School of Management, her focus was joining a company where she could grow and with a prestigious reputation befitting all those years of study and sacrifice.

So, when she was offered a position at McKinsey & Company, it didn't even occur to her to negotiate. It was never about the money.

"I was just excited to be there," Titi recalled.

Fortunately for Titi, McKinsey's entry-level pay was relatively standardized because those first years after business school can be critical. According to the *Wall Street Journal,* which analyzed US data for 2015 and 2016 college graduates, the pay gap between men and women emerges within three years of entering the workforce.[3] And it rarely gets closed. When you start at the low end of the scale, it is hard to catch up. Women still earn only 84 cents for every dollar a man makes. A typical 10% to 20% increase with each promotion or review won't get you there. Being aware of this issue – even before you enter the workforce – could help prevent us from falling behind.

Sallie Krawcheck, one of the highest-ranking women ever to work on Wall Street, has dedicated herself to closing the gender wealth gap as founder of Ellevest, a digital investment platform run by women, for women. The former CEO of Merrill Lynch Wealth Management, Sanford Bernstein, Smith Barney, and former CFO of Citigroup sees the financial disparity in broader and much starker terms. It's not just the pay gap, but the investment wealth gap that impacts women and holds back their potential:

"The gender wealth gap is the bigger deal," she shared on a recent Russell Reynolds Associates' *Redefiners* podcast. "Globally, women only possess 32 cents to a white man's dollar; and for Black women, it's only a penny."

In addition to earning less than men, women also reach their peak salaries at a younger age than men do, they take more career breaks, and they tend to live longer than men. And, while there are plenty of exceptions, women on average are 2.5 years younger than their partners, which can create a distorted perspective on which parent should step out of the workforce to focus more on children, for example. Those kinds of decisions, which fail to take in the whole picture of her potentiality, can also hobble a woman's earning power.

This lack of overall wealth has implications beyond being able to retire comfortably. Without that growing nest egg, women won't feel as empowered to leave a toxic relationship or move on from a job that doesn't fulfill them.

"If you want to improve society and make it fairer, get more money into the hands of women," Sallie said. "It's a known fact that in developed economies women's families are better off, nonprofits do well, and everyone's existence improves. So wealth disparity is hurting us all." For Sallie, the answer is to encourage more women to take control of their own investing.

Titi has also become a strong advocate for financial literacy, particularly among young girls. To that end, she supports the nonprofit Invest in Girls, Inc., a program of the Council for Economic Education that exposes girls to financial concepts and mentors them in partnership with professional and executive women in financial services.

"It starts with good old-fashioned financial education for boys and girls," Titi explained.

A foundational level of financial literacy – understanding the basics like assets, liabilities, how to invest in yourself, the pros and cons of student loans and car loans – normalizes conversations about money and removes some of the stigma that has traditionally surrounded the topic for women and girls.

"What I have tried to do is encourage girls to lean into financial literacy and to recognize that money is neither inherently good nor bad. It is a tool that can help them to achieve other goals."

Fierce Independence

Knowledge and desire for financial independence can be especially powerful when seeded at a young age, and I can speak about this from personal experience. My mother grew up in a dysfunctional home where money was scarce. My grandfather was an alcoholic who couldn't keep a steady job. Seeing how much my grandmother suffered, always anxious about keeping a roof over her children's heads and their bellies full, deeply impacted my mother's outlook. She never entertained the same Cinderella fantasies that many women of her generation had, where the prince would come along and take care of her. And she was determined that her own daughter would grow up to be an independent, self-sufficient woman. It was all about having a career of significance, with serious earning potential.

"Never rely on a man or anyone else – you need to stand on your own two feet," she told me, repeatedly.

My mother and my father both sacrificed to pay for me to have a world-class education. But it was my mom especially who imbued in me the self-confidence to be brave and to do anything I wanted to do in life. She reminded me weekly – if not daily – that the only thing that could stop me would be my own self-imposed mental constraints. "Don't ever say you can't – you *can,* and *you* will!" was her often-uttered mantra to me.

My mother's words have been burned into my brain. Never one to complain or to be passive, my mother showed me, through her own indefatigable work ethic, that when things don't go my way, the best course of action is to shake off the setback, be resilient, and go after anything that matters to me.

Then again, grit is not always enough. Having options requires a level of self-sufficiency and that comes from financial security.

Always knowing you'll have money in the bank to pay your bills will embolden you to make career moves that take you further rather than staying in a job that doesn't fulfill you out of fear.

Although we have some catching up to do in the workplace, it is within our power to get what we are actually worth, versus what many of us may *think* we are worth. It will require a shift in mindset, and a determination to ascend not just through job titles, but fair financial compensation. Of course, there is an art to the ask.

Money Talks

Getting comfortable talking about money, taking the negative associations out of it, needs to happen early. We tend to associate asking for our worth with greed. Similarly, women have historically been encouraged to focus more on purpose and peacemaking at home than ambition and amassing wealth in careers on Wall Street. We have also been acculturated to smile, get along, not be too uppity, and focus on the well-being of others. But here's the thing: building wealth inures to us and to the ultimate benefit of our family and community.

While money isn't everything and there is tremendous value in having a sense of purpose, we tend to overcorrect. The result is that we often shy away from careers that are more lucrative.

Titi challenges this thinking: "Why not look for a career that allows you to monetize your value? You are not a volunteer. You have every right to earn what you are worth. There is no reason not to choose an industry where you get paid well, and whatever industry you choose, don't suboptimize your potential by staying in situations where you are underpaid or undervalued."

Until women and men are on level ground financially, there can be no true equality. Without financial parity, we will always be economically dependent in some way because, in this world, money is power. "Women have got to deprogram themselves and ask for what they are worth," Titi told me.

It's time to ask ourselves why we can't seem to get past our own squeamishness over the money conversation. If we can't unlock the reasons why, which can go all the way back to the way we were raised and how our parents approached money, then we can at least come up with new narratives to get us to where we need to go. "Figure out the mental framework and get comfortable with it," said Titi. "In my case, it's about creating generational opportunity."

For many women, making it about others, rather than themselves, is one construct that can work. Personally, I get it. I'm a beast when it comes to negotiating on behalf of others, but I likely would not be quite so forthright about my own compensation if I wasn't driven by the comfort and well-being of my own children and the nonprofit organizations I enjoy contributing to financially.

However you think about money, psychologically it's crucial to push past any mindset that might hold you back. It's not a wise long-term strategy to tell ourselves to keep our heads down and accept whatever we're given.

In 2021, I had a candidate who was eager to take the job even though the remuneration package they were offering was two standard deviations below the rest of the market. I just couldn't let that happen. So I went back to the client and explained that I'd already done 15 searches for similar kinds of companies and warned them it would not be long before other recruiters – not me – would be approaching her with offers that would remind her of just how grossly underpaid she was.

"She may love this job now," I told them. "But 18 months or two years from now those calls are going to come. Do you really want to take that risk? Do you really want an unhappy person distracted by these numbers? Compensation is not something she should have to think about every day. She just needs to trust that it's fair so that she can put it out of her mind and think about her job and perform to the best of her ability. It's good for her, and it's good for the company."

Thankfully, they saw my point.

Showing Up

But it's not just conversation that will enable you to ask for more. It's conduct. How you carry yourself impacts how you are seen by those who are in a position to assign a number to our worth. When you truly believe your value, it reflects in your actions. Titi calls this "showing up."

She has observed in meetings, for example, how women quickly move into the role of note-taking or organizing logistics and administrative details, often because they are asked to take on these responsibilities, or they feel a subtle pressure to do so. Titi advises these women to resist and not raise their hands for all the administrative tasks because, no matter what her position or actual responsibilities, she will soon be perceived as the caretaker.

"Don't fall into that trap; don't take on these caretaker roles, because caretakers do not get the highest pay. Nobody ever rewards you for that kind of service. The caretaker is not thought of as the future of the enterprise."

Instead, be intentional about *how* you present yourself. "If you want to be taken seriously, you've got to show up seriously."

Titi also advises women to do more than just their day job. This could mean getting involved in projects and causes you care about and giving yourself opportunities to meet and be seen by senior leaders and other people of influence in the organization in another context. Let them hear you speak about an industry issue. Show them how impressive you truly are. Putting your head down and performing your job to the highest level, hoping they will notice and reward you with a bigger paycheck, is wishful thinking. It doesn't typically work that way.

Getting involved in industry associations and other organizations outside your company is essential for building up your external network. Internal connectedness matters, of course. Cultivating relationships within your company and across functions is one way to be seen. But it's not enough. Whether it relates to attaining a new position or higher income, stepping outside those four walls will help you see your worth within the context of the whole marketplace. It can shake you out of your rut and help those around you see you in a new light. Just as in any relationship, we tend to take those closest to us for granted. Sometimes it takes someone outside your immediate circle to notice your many attributes to remind those who should already appreciate your worth.

Don't limit yourself by not knowing enough people. Being savvy about your industry and having a broad relationship network can make you more effective in your role. And, to Titi's point about showing up, when you are in a meeting and able to bring up a fact or observation about what is going on in your industry outside the company itself, your senior leaders will notice. These external connections help you see beyond your immediate environment and bring invaluable information that can further your career and help you in negotiating your financial package.

Take My Call

External networking includes taking calls from recruiters. Information is power, and the best way to know what you are worth is to ask someone who negotiates compensation packages for a living. Who else can you ask to gather objective and fact-based intelligence specific to your role? Titi is someone who picks up the phone when executive recruiters call, even when she's not looking to change jobs. It's a way to build relationships, perhaps introduce someone in her network to the opportunity, stay abreast of the marketplace, and stay in the conversation.

But even if you are not at that stage in your career – if you are only just partially on your road to senior leadership, you can still get some idea of the range from online forums like Glassdoor, for example, in which employees anonymously post reviews and salary information about their companies. I know a group of senior-level women from the same company who get together for lunch every year around bonus time. They put their numbers in a hat with no names attached, pull them out one by one, and discuss. I'd like to think there are groups of women within many companies who are looking out for each other in similar ways.

But if you haven't thought of these strategies until now, don't despair. You may have missed out on some earning years, but it's never too late to change your income trajectory. Consider Kat Cole, president, chief operating officer, and board director of Athletic Greens, a rapidly growing global health and nutrition company. Kat was most recently president and COO of Focus Brands, overseeing the company's nine presidents and brands like Cinnabon, generating billions in sales around the world, and she has angel-invested in more than 60 early and growth-stage consumer and wellness companies. She was also a Young

Global Leader of the World Economic Forum. She comes from a blue-collar background and is the first college-educated member of her family.

Financial literacy was an alien concept to Kat when growing up. Yet she always understood the value of a hard-earned dollar. At just 9 years old, she took whatever odd jobs she could in her Jacksonville, Florida, neighborhood, from clearing leaves and branches off roofs to delivering newspapers to babysitting, supplementing her single working mother's meager income to help put food on the table for her two younger siblings. At 17, when she was finally of legal age to draw a paycheck, Kat took a job as a hostess at the local branch of Hooters, an international chain of restaurants, working every shift she could between college classes.

Getting paid and maximizing her income by figuring out what made customers happy and therefore more generous with their tips made her feel empowered. Kat shucked oysters and cracked crab legs, engaging her dining patrons with her infectious personality to the point where her waitressing money belt was bursting with cash. Earning that cash by working hard and smart gave the budding leader and entrepreneur a rush. "Nothing felt better to me than having that paycheck in my hands," Kat shared with me.

After a lifetime of struggle, a steady paycheck meant options and, above all, self-sufficiency. Her mother, who'd left Kat's alcoholic father and took a leap into the unknown, never wanted her daughter to be in the same desperate position. Kat saved, kept her expenses low, and never relied on credit, so that she would always have a nest egg.

"My mom built into me this notion that I had to be independent at all costs. She did not want me depending on anyone or anything. If I wanted something, great, but she didn't want me to need it, so that was always at the back of my mind."

For years throughout her career, that approach helped give Kat the agency and courage to follow her gut and leap into the next big challenge. She continued working at Hooters, learning every aspect of the business, from front-of-house service to dealing with vendors, to the point where her expertise and ability to lead got her noticed by top management. As the company expanded, they sent her all over the world to open new locations. When she was sent by the company on her first business trip, to Sydney, Kat didn't even have a passport.

But with each promotion, it never occurred to her to question the compensation package they offered. "Education was my currency," Kat recalled. "I loved having all those opportunities to learn."

By the age of 20, she'd gone from shift work to more managerial roles in the corporate office, where she initially gave up a level of income to professionalize her career. Every two years she was promoted, and she took what they offered. "I was just thrilled to be there."

Find Your Script

It wasn't until she reached a director role that it even occurred to her to push back and question what the pay scale might be in similar roles at other companies. She did her research; by then she had developed a network through her involvement in various industry forums and associations to have some sense of what was both competitive and fair. She was also keenly self-aware. Kat brought an extraordinary amount of relationship capital and technical knowledge to each new role, having performed so many different jobs at the company – experience at a level that few in the industry possessed. Armed with this information, she developed a tactful yet effective way of getting her point across. She informed them what similar roles were being paid in other companies, then said:

"Look, I am not trying to take advantage here. I know you want me to feel good about the value I am creating." Kat was subtle, weaving it into the conversation in a matter-of-fact way that let them know she knew. "It was my way of saying, without threatening, don't let me find out you are paying someone else in a similar role more."

The more you tackle the remuneration question head on, the better you become at the art of the ask. Over the years, the young executive grew increasingly skillful at these conversations. She had long since overcome her bashfulness. The stakes were more complex as she rose, involving equity and bonuses by the time she reached the senior executive level. The more of these negotiations she went through, the more she saw how well her managers received her straightforward approach.

She had already been encouraging her direct reports, mostly women, to have those same conversations. Through her various industry board roles, including leading a compensation committee, she also coached women outside her organization. It made her realize that this hesitance over financial negotiations was endemic.

"I love helping people appreciate where they are in their journey, understanding their experience curve, the market for their work, and how they should see this in terms of their total compensation."

Of course, it's often a lot easier to do this for others than for yourself. The stakes were especially high when Kat made the move from a vice president at the restaurant chain to president of Cinnabon, one of the leading brands owned by Focus Group. It was a huge leap in responsibility as well as a whole new floor in terms of salary, bonus, equity, and benefits. Kat understood the importance of getting this right, because undervaluing herself could impact her earning power in the years to come.

Although she appreciated that she was less experienced than the other brand presidents and would be running the smallest brand in the parent company's stable, she also realized that there was a standard amount that the position was worth. The problem was that by this point in her career she had never seriously considered leaving her old company and had not had the opportunity for meaningful conversations with recruiters, so she had no idea what that number would be. She was bold enough to come right out and ask the CEO what the other presidents were being paid.

"There was nothing uncomfortable or awkward about the question," Kat recalled.

Her new boss explained how compensation worked in the organization and gave her a range. Kat accepted that she would be on the lower end but made a deal with him that they would revisit her compensation in 90 days so she could hopefully land more solidly in the middle of that range, depending upon how she performed in the new role. Sure enough, she got the raise.

It's worth noting here that often the real gains people get are pay increases when they move companies because that "resets" the floor. People who remain at the same company for a long time tend to be underpaid relative to the market. In fact, both women and men who stay in the same company for more than two years earn up to 50% less over their lifetimes.

Pay Raise Pro

Kat's accumulated experience with these negotiations created such fluency in the subject that, by the time Focus created a new strategic role just for her, with no industry benchmarks for pay, she was undeterred. With a staff of two and no major brand attached to it, it wasn't obvious or easy to explain the magnitude or importance of what she would be doing for the company. So, Kat did for herself what she'd counseled others to do, taking a deep dive to understand what her new role was truly worth. She made the pitch, explaining how critical and strategic her division would be in terms of restructuring the entire business, and the impact she would have. Kat was so convincing, she reached a whole new level of pay and equity within the business.

In a nutshell, she told them, "You don't want me to be distracted by money because it's a dumbass thing to be distracted by when we are trying to build an empire here. Just make it good enough that I don't have to worry about it."

She did her homework, asked for what was fair, then took it to the bank.

Compensation is a multifaceted area, and certainly not black and white. When helping my clients and candidates to arrive at a compensation package that both sides can view with equanimity, I encourage them to take the following four factors under advisement:

1. Where the candidate is today: Although some women are currently undercompensated relative to their male peers, you still need to consider what the candidate is making today (in states where that can be legally asked). The vast majority of the time, people are not going to take on the risk of going to a new job without a pay raise of at least 15–20%.

2. Compression issues at the company: Large public companies will have different salary bands and compensation schema than, for example, pre-IPO start-ups, which will generally be equity-richer and cash-poorer. Consider what other similarly leveled people at the company you are going to are getting paid, as you'll likely want to maintain some parity with those individuals.

3. Industry benchmarks: Look at other similarly sized companies, in your particularly industry, in the same location to determine what is "market" for this position today.

4. Psychological elements: There is a happiness factor when it comes to accepting a new job, and you need to reflect on what it will take for you to excitedly jump out of bed every morning to go do this new job.

Put all four of those considerations together in a proverbial martini shaker and ruminate on them. You should try to put all of the data you have at your fingertips into a spreadsheet so you can consider them with as little emotion as possible. Build out a four-year, year-over-year compensation grid that compares your current cash flow with your expected cash flow at the new employer. Objectively leverage this data to show the company where you are today and how your equity and cash compensation line up going forward.

* * *

Your Path to the Top Checklist

Pick a career or an industry that pays. Purpose is all well and good, but it's possible to find a culture and company with values that match your own in a job that also rewards you financially. You are not a volunteer. You deserve to be paid well for your hard work and brilliance.

Financial literacy = independence. Even if you missed out on financial education and topics like IRAs, assets, investing, and equity were not part of your family's dinner conversation, it's never too late to start. The more you know, the more you can build your wealth, and that will give you options so that you never have to depend on someone else.

Find a way to frame it. Make it about someone else, like your kids, if that works for you. Or pretend you're advocating on behalf of your best friend. Whatever you tell yourself, you need to get comfortable with the conversation, fast. If not, you may find yourself on the edge of a growing pay chasm.

Arm yourself with facts. Information is power *and* money. When you're negotiating for your next position, do the research first. Reach out to recruiters, a trusted colleague or industry peer, or investigate online to get a sense of the pay ranges for your role and industry. Lean on the data throughout the conversation so it is fact-based, not emotion-driven (for either side).

Show up with intention. Don't let them see you take on a subservient role. If you join a task force, make sure it's a position that will help propel your compensation forward, not a random special project no one really cares about or values. Handmaiden tasks are underappreciated and diminish your value in the eyes of the top leadership. Conduct yourself like the boss you are.

Network, network, network. Whether internally, among other women leaders, or any affinity group, and especially externally among industry peers, you will be able to see your role and its financial worth in a broader context. When demonstrated in a meeting or casual conversation in the break room, that extra knowledge will also help you to stand out to people of influence within your organization.

If not you, then who? It's our turn to set up the next generation, and that starts with setting up yourself, so go for it!

CHAPTER 6

Up, Not Out

CHAPTER 6

Up, Not Out

*[My mother] had handed down respect for the
possibilities – and the will to grasp them.*

—Alice Walker

From the time she was an undergraduate at Carleton University in Ottawa, Canada, Donna Morris, whom we first met back in Chapter 3, knew exactly what she wanted to do. A summer job assisting the director of pensions and benefits in the HR department at the City of Ottawa revealed that she could combine her two passions: helping others develop their skill sets, and business. Under the guidance of her boss and first mentor, she became laser-focused, pursuing the Canadian Certified Human Resources Professional (CHRP) designation and intentionally building specialized skills and seizing every opportunity that came her way. Today, Donna is arguably one of the most powerful human resource executives in the world as chief people officer of Walmart, where she is responsible for the professional and personal well-being of 2.3 million employees in 24 countries. To reach that level, Donna made few compromises in her career, leading her into the highest ranks of the global retail giant. But she did not compromise on what mattered to her just as much as building her career: having a family.

Early in her career, Donna vowed to herself that she would have *both* motherhood and a successful career. There was never any debate in her mind about giving up one for the other.

"When people ask about the accomplishment I'm most proud of, it would absolutely be that I am a mom to our now adult son, Kyle, and that I have also always held a full-time job outside the home. It was not always easy to integrate work and life, but the personal and professional rewards far outweigh any regrets."

Starting a family had some devastating moments. Her first child was born with a rare genetic disorder. The infant had a heart condition and the doctors told Donna that, if her child survived the neonatal intensive care unit, she would be blind and have other life-changing health complications. As a new mom along with her husband, they vowed to be the best parents they could be and, whatever challenges they would face, they would overcome. *I'm going to be your mom,* Donna whispered to this precious being as she lay sleeping in her hospital crib. But her daughter never left the hospital. A month later, she passed away.

"It was the lightning rod that changed how my life turned out," Donna shared with me.

The young couple did not give up, despite facing the risk of the same tragic outcome. When she became pregnant with her son, all Donna could do was "cross my fingers and pray" that this child would be healthy. He was. But this experience of starting a family was a lesson in resilience. Donna realized she had the "grit and grind" to power through any setback. This fire test of motherhood gave her the strength not only to be a great mom, but an inspiring leader who could instill that same perspective and confidence in those around her, including Kyle.

It came full circle when Kyle shared with his mother that she was a wonderful role model to him and to how he viewed women in the workplace. After years of the all-too-common maternal guilt about missing baseball, hockey and soccer games and feeling the tug and pull of late nights at the office when she might have been home reading him a bedtime story, Donna learned that Kyle was as career driven as his mom.

Of course, Donna should not be considered a unicorn. But one of the biggest obstacles to parity at the top is the fact that women often press pause in the prime of their careers to start a family, only to find that doors are closed to them when they are ready to return to the workforce. It is as if everything we accomplished prior to having children has evaporated. I know because I have seen it play out countless times as a leadership advisor.

The Gap Years

I started thinking about writing this book many years ago when I was a young associate at RRA. At that time, and still today, I would occasionally have "courtesy interviews" with job seekers. Often the person I met with would be a woman who had left the workforce about a decade earlier to raise her children. Then her partner left the family; or became sick, disabled, or died; or found that his job prospects had declined significantly. Or her kids were at school full time, so she had less to do at home and missed comradery and intellectual stimulation, and yes, the paycheck and independence. When these women sat down with me, they wanted to know how to get back into the workforce.

The truth that I could never bring myself to say out loud was that their journey back into corporate America would be nearly impossible. And if they did manage to get back in, they would likely never achieve the same financial success that they could have gained had they never stepped off their career path in the first place.

Occasionally I would get a follow-up note from one of the women, letting me know their progress. Most often, if they were able to find paying work, they were working as an hourly consultant for someone who, at one point, had been much more junior to them. I couldn't help but feel not only frustrated at the system, but also that these women had felt forced to make a binary choice between stepping off altogether or not being the kind of parent that they wanted to be. Many of them compromised their own career ambitions for those of their partners, for countless reasons. But what if there were a better way – for everyone? What if our corporate structure provided the tools, along with the managerial and organizational support to be fully present both for our careers *and* our families?

Fast forward to the spring of 2022. A few months before embarking on this book, I received an out-of-office message from a male colleague whose wife had just had their second child. He was about to go on paternity leave. His message served to alert folks that he would not be responding to their email any time soon. He went on to list all the things that he would be helping to facilitate in his household while on leave: "Over the next month," he informed us, "I will be helping my wife as she recovers from her C-section, taking care of our newborn, driving our two-year-old to preschool and helping her transition into her new role of big sister, and trying to be a present father and husband."

I loved that. Yet I couldn't help but notice that his email was unconsciously echoing what women have been trying to justify for decades. It was also a timely reminder that my goal here is not only to help women be empowered to live their best lives, but to help their partners do the same. Just as women shouldn't have to explain why they want to continue working, men in our country shouldn't have to explain if they are full-time fathers, husbands, or partners.

Many other more socially advanced countries have already figured out this puzzle. In fact, the United States ranks lowest in the world among the 41 industrialized nations in terms of paid leave for fathers, with zero weeks required. In fact, the US is the *only* one among these nations not to have mandated paid paternity leave,[1] and that must change. Having preordained, archaic, typecast-gendered roles does no favors for either men or women in helping them lead their most fulfilled lives at home and in the workplace.

False Assumptions

Our workplace structures are modeled on centuries-old precepts. They were put in place even before the industrial age, based largely on male workers' abilities. They were plowing fields or building things that took raw strength. In the industrial age, a company's success was predicated on getting hundreds – if not thousands – of workers to commute to a factory to build a product, to work as cogs in the machine for a set period of time. And today that male bias still exists. (Even the formula for US office temperatures—developed in the 1960s—was based on the metabolic rate of an average 40-year-old man.)[2]

Today, our economy has evolved. There is no longer any X- or Y-chromosome-based reason why women should not be as powerful – or as financially successful – as men. If every woman had the choice to be simultaneously career-minded and family-centric, we might create a world where men and women were financial equals. When women feel that they need to take a backseat to their partners (or anyone), whether by choice or because of the false assumptions of society, family, or peers, we are robbing our society of progress, creativity, and brilliance.

That does not mean there won't be trade-offs. Time and again, Donna Morris had to endure the disapproving stares of colleagues at her previous company when she chose to drop her son off at school in the mornings.

"When I wasn't traveling, I wanted to have that responsibility," Donna shared with me. "I wanted to start off my morning giving my son a squeeze and telling him to have a great day."

But after getting through the carpool line, seeing her child safely out of the car and on his way up to the school, then finding a parking spot so that she could dial into the 8:30 a.m. meetings (which she never missed), "I always felt a little like I was in the penalty box."

Looking back, "That should not have happened, and many of us are starting to say, 'This is NOT ok,'" said Donna. "It should not be assumed that the only way to get it done is to be in the same physical space as everyone else."

It is a recurring theme I have been hearing from dozens of successful female leaders with whom I have been speaking since remote work became not just a thing, but *the* thing. Although we already had the tools to work remotely, Covid forced us to use them. For so many of us who had been conflicted about the balance between life at home and work, working from home became the ultimate epiphany that we could succeed on our own terms.

Donna's one regret was that she, or any woman on a career and leadership track, ever had to put up with those periods of self-doubt in the first place.

"Much of the perception has been, 'Okay, if I really want to take those next steps in my life and start a family, I am going to have to sacrifice my career goals.' Yet I have never, not once, had a man tell me that."

Many of these executives and managers, even today, see it as an either/or situation. Again, they believe the choice must be binary.

"I have had women in their late 30s and early 40s tell me they chose not to get married because they really wanted to have a C-suite role," Donna told me. "Or they turn down a job because they want to get pregnant and they are dealing with fertility treatments, in vitro, et cetera."

Donna's response has been to counsel these women, assuring them they can do both, and that they will have her full support in whatever role they choose to take on. She is intentional in her communication, listening carefully and working to build trust, so that the individuals in her organization can feel comfortable expressing themselves with full candor. As Donna points out, "For every time someone has shared her life situation and doubts with me, there live countless more individuals who felt like they could not have those discussions, and they are left to put their career or life choices to the side."

Even in the most progressive organizations, moms face profound internal struggles over how to reconcile their professional and personal lives. Self-doubt goes with the territory. Agnes Heftberger has spent her entire career with IBM, where she is now general manager and technology leader for Southeast Asia, Australia, New Zealand, and Korea, based in Singapore. The self-described "lifer" has been given every opportunity to thrive at the 111-year-old tech icon, with bosses and mentors who have believed in her ever since she took her first internship while studying at Vienna University in Austria. But, when she became pregnant with her first child in 2018, she had concerns.

"I remember driving into work the morning I had to tell my boss that I was pregnant. I was dreading that conversation. At the same time, I told my mother that my career as I knew it was over."

"It wasn't that I had been given a reason to worry that IBM or my boss wouldn't be supportive. I'd just seen so many friends at other companies stop their careers, so I assumed I would need to make that choice too. In the end, all that worrying was completely unwarranted. My boss was understanding and reassuring. I told him I wanted to come back eight weeks after giving birth (the legal maternity leave in Germany) and he agreed. He said I could come back to the same position, take more time, or try something new – it was all up to me."

But five months into Agnes's pregnancy, and with every intention of going back to her old role after eight weeks on maternity leave, she learned that her boss would be taking on a new role at IBM. For a moment, the news threw the expectant mother into another panic. "The replacement wasn't yet in place and I wasn't sure if they would honor the agreement I had and give me my old job back," she told me.

Much to her surprise, IBM did one better, and made *her* the boss. She became vice president in charge of sales for Germany, Switzerland, and Austria – a highly demanding position. Her boss made a point of announcing to all associates in the German-speaking market that he chose Agnes because he was "fundamentally convinced" that she was the best candidate for the role. Running the communication by her first, he detailed how the transition would happen, and who would be filling in while she was on leave and partner with her as she took over the position. He was transparent about the fact that she was about to become a new mom – and that the management team was looking forward to supporting her in being successful both in that role and in finding balance as a mother." It was a statement to the organization that a new standard had been set.

"It was one of those confirmational moments where I knew I was in the right place."

That level of support is still not as common as it should be. But, as I write this, something is beginning to shift – in ways we could not have imagined before March 2020. We now have options, brought to light by this new way of working and transparency.

"The fact that we are having these discussions means that people have become more liberated in the last two years," Donna observed. "And it is for us as leaders to at least help people talk. Let's focus on emotional and mental well-being. Let's make sure people feel psychologically safe to share what they need to be successful."

The Cage Match

That's not where I was mentally when I first learned I was pregnant. I could not imagine how my career would not take a serious blow. Not only would I need to manage the physical tribulations of pregnancy, but I feared taking maternity leave could put me at a competitive disadvantage. I had convinced myself that my firm would be, at best, annoyed that I would be stepping off the hamster wheel to produce something besides client receivables.

To be clear, this wasn't about my firm or its policies – this was about my own perception of how people would look at me pregnant, as if I were no longer "all in." It didn't help that nearly every day, some random person would ask me, "Are you going back to work after you have the baby?" So many people asked me that irritating albeit well-intentioned question that I eventually just started responding jokingly, "I was planning to maybe take a day or two off at first."

Looking back, I didn't handle that first maternity leave as well as I could have. Despite my colleagues being incredibly supportive, I was still fearful that I would lose my standing as a superstar at work. In the back of my mind I kept wondering if people would forget about me, and if I would forever be passed over for promotions or interesting work opportunities because they surreptitiously took issue with my motherhood and decried my family being a priority over work. In retrospect, this might seem silly, but I assure you that it was a very real and present paranoia of mine. For this reason, even while my son was fiercely latching onto my nipples during my maternity leave, I found myself logging onto my work email, eager to be immediately responsive to clients and to help colleagues. While I was physically out of the office, intellectually and emotionally, I never cut the cord.

Once I was back in the office after my maternity leave, imagine my surprise when a) it felt like I hadn't missed a single thing, and b) I now felt more in sync with the vast majority of my clients with children. We now had something in common, something to bond over, and something that made us more like peers than we had ever been. In addition to our various titles at work, we were also parents. Much to my complete shock, having children seemed to be a net positive to my vocation. Having a child humanized me, metamorphosizing me into a full-fledged adult. It was as if I'd gained admission into a special club.

Maintaining my working mom title was sometimes a tricky balance. Living an hour-plus commute from my office in traffic, I would always attempt to leave the city by 5 p.m. to get home by 6 p.m. to spend an hour with my son before putting him to bed at 7 p.m. But one evening, when he was about six months old, I got caught up on client calls and could not extract myself at my usual departure time. Frantic to see my baby, I finally extricated myself an hour later, then drove like mad to get home to hold him in my arms again, missing him so much after having been away from him for 12 hours.

I was nearly there, careening into my garage, and I could see my husband opening the door to the kitchen for me – almost like in slow-motion – with my son all bundled in his swaddle, when my cell phone rang. I reflexively answered, and it was a client wanting to talk to me. I looked at the clock on my dashboard. It was 6:55. He said, "Do you have a minute?" I laughed, probably because I was nervous, and I said, "Actually, I don't right now. Could I call you in 30?" I explained that I was rushing to tuck my newborn into bed, and he was entirely understanding about it.

Of course, you might wonder why I would even pick up the phone. But at the time, I had been so unilaterally focused on career achievement, it was my Pavlovian response. There wasn't even a decision to make. The client came first. In an instant, the two most important spheres of my life – work and family – were juxtaposed against each other as if in a cage match, in a seemingly zero-sum game. There would be a winner, and there would be a loser. But in that moment I knew that the loser could not be – and would not be – my son.

It couldn't be me, either. I didn't bring a child into this world not to experience every important moment in his life – and not to get the inexplicable and intoxicating pleasures of being a parent. Snuggling in bed, reading stories, playing Legos on the floor, going to soccer games, organizing birthday parties: I wanted it all. So I became determined to be the best mother *and* executive I could be.

It was working pretty well. While out on maternity leave with my son, I was promoted. Three years later in 2010, I gave birth to a baby girl, and I was promoted yet again, this time to partner at my firm, a significant achievement in the life of a professional services executive. But in 2013, I would face one additional cage match, when my then-three-year-old daughter was diagnosed with a brain tumor. My firm and clients could not have been more supportive. They showed up for me. *Anything you need, Jenna*, my colleagues, management, and partners in their various ways, told me. *We've got you.*

I was also hyper-present. I was in full mama-bear mode for my little girl, making sure I found the best brain surgeon on the planet to operate on her. I worked the phones, leveraging my ample network to learn everything about best treatments and outcomes from experts in the field. I used all my professional, diplomatic, and leadership skills to beg, plead, and cajole the country's top pediatric neurosurgeon to cut short his Caribbean vacation to fly home to perform the urgent operation, which he mercifully did.

Yet Pavlov's dog kept yapping in my year. After nine hours of delicate surgery, which was a resounding success, I was sitting next to my unconscious, intubated baby girl in recovery when my phone vibrated. It was a client, and I automatically picked up the call. The attending physician was horrified.

"Ms. Fisher, your daughter is about to wake up! You need to put down that phone and hold her hand!"

"Oh, yes, of course!" I replied, snapping back into the moment. "I've gotta go now, I'll call you back!"

It took enormous reserves of personal will and emotional and physical energy to be all things to everyone. Some might even say I put too much pressure on myself to be all things to all people. Yet my career is robust and, most important, my daughter is healthy and happy.

I am living a fortunate life full of love and support, positive role models and opportunities. My parents told me I could do anything or be anything I chose. I married a man who cares about my career as much as he cares for his own. But what I have come to realize is that although I've been lucky, I am not so extraordinary that other people can't have it all too.

Bait and Switch

A law school classmate of mine who was among the top handful of graduates from my class chose to join a prestigious global law firm on the basis that it had a "Grow or Go" model, meaning that there was no set timetable for making partner – you could take as much or as little time as you wanted to get there, so long as you were performing and growing professionally. Although my friend was still single when she was hired, it was no secret that, in addition to her burning professional ambition, she was eager to one day start a family. This program seemed to take the psychic pressure off young mothers trying to "do it all," so my friend was excited to launch her career there.

Three years into her law firm tenure, she was a top decile performer, and all signs pointed towards her eventual ascent to partner. She eventually did become pregnant and shared with her boss that she wanted to opt into Grow or Go. Imagine her surprise when she was met with derision and was told that she would never make partner if she opted for that alternative path. My friend was crushed and made the decision not to return to this law firm – or any other – after she gave birth to her beautiful son.

Stories like this are all too common. What a waste for both parties. The short-sighted firm lost out on a major talent, and my friend had to forgo considerable income-earning potential as well. Her experience made me even more convinced that there needs to be a better, more enlightened way for businesses to operate.

Long-Term Vision

It all begins with a plan. Just as you must look at the business units and companies you work for with long-term vision, so you must view the arc and scope of your own professional and personal life. My grandmother always said, paraphrasing Benjamin Franklin, "If you fail to plan, you plan to fail."

I have been a consummate planner since an early age. Growing up as an only child, I had a lot of time alone to daydream about what I wanted my future to look like, and I have been keeping a daily journal since I started writing at age four. Several years ago, I had the opportunity to look through some of those tomes that are hidden away in banker boxes in my attic. It was exciting to go back in time and realize that I had put together surprisingly accurate and elaborate timelines of what my adult life would look like. I had somehow made prognostications worthy of Nostradamus, listing which years I would complete various graduate schools, get engaged, get married, move to California, buy a house, get a dog, get promoted at work, and yes, have children. Other than actualizing the boy-girl twins that I had been planning on having for most of my youth, nearly all my other plans have not only been fulfilled, but exceeded.

Having a long-term mindset will allow you to continue on your trajectory up, and not out of, the workforce. Should you decide to take some time for raising your family, planning ahead will allow you at least to keep a toe in the water. You can set yourself up to work part time, as a consultant or entrepreneur in the field to which you eventually want to return. Be strategic about it, so that when you have a meeting with someone like me, you can point to recent experience with confidence.

But don't fall into the trap of becoming too rigid. Sometimes you need to reroute. Back in 1994, I thought that business school was reserved solely for men who wanted to work in financial services on Wall Street. I just didn't see myself fitting in with that club, and I wasn't particularly interested in banking, derivatives, hedge funds, private equity, or venture capital, and I always thought that to be great at something, you must have a passion for it. So I quickly dismissed the thought of business school and instead went to law school. I had spent time on Capitol Hill during my college summers, interning at environmental nonprofits, and I thought that my strong writing, research, and skills of persuasion would be well suited for a legal career. I wasn't wrong, exactly, and although I loved the dynamic and spirited conversations that took place in law school, I found that the actual practice of corporate law was not quite as good a fit for my personality and interests as I had hoped.

After attending law school, when I found myself working at Bain & Company and contemplating going to business school, part of me felt like a failure because that had not been on "The Plan." Going to business school would delay my ambitions for promotion, marriage, and children by two years. At the ripe old age of 27, I feared I was becoming too advanced in years to go back to school (which seems ridiculous now!). But I knew that the most important thing at that point in my life was to set myself up for a long, happy career. I felt the need to get my education under my belt so I wouldn't have regrets or allow any options to foreclose on me.

My point is that, with some slight detours, the long-range vision worked out for me. I am grateful that I always innately understood how to organize myself and how to imagine and manifest the life I wanted for myself. I once heard the phrase "Learn in your 20s, earn in your 30s." All this methodical planning set me up by the end of my 20s to be ready for the next step.

Setting Up for Success

Titi Cole, CEO of Legacy Franchises at Citigroup whom we met in Chapter 5, is a fellow consummate planner. She shared with me how the financial services industry "has not always been kind to working moms," but she figured it out. She took certain steps in her working and personal life to make sure that, even as a busy executive, she would not miss the important things in her children's lives. One of those moves involved a career change. Her earlier role as a consultant at McKinsey required her to travel, often weekly, so she made the switch into banking, which, while extremely demanding and requiring long hours, at least allowed her to get home most evenings in time to tuck her two sons into bed or ask about their days at school when they were all gathered at the family dinner table. She was still putting in the long hours, but she was doing so on her terms.

"You have to think about a career that is conducive to the kind of life you want," Titi explained. "I wanted to be involved in my kids' lives every day. I was able to protect and guard the things that were sacred to me. I was happy to work after they went to bed."

Titi was also intentional about *when* she had her kids.

"I wanted to start my family before the age of 30 and be a young empty nester, not wait until I was at a certain stage in my career."

Once Titi envisioned the life and career she wanted, she put all the elements in place that were necessary to make it happen. "I am a ruthless outsourcer," Titi told me.

She did the math and prioritized her personal resources to invest in the highest-quality childcare she could afford, even if that meant living in a smaller home, because she never wanted to have to worry that her children were not getting their needs met.

"I was paying more for their caregiver than I was for my mortgage. Spend your money on childcare that gives you peace of mind. Over time, our nanny became a house manager so I could be with my kids on the weekend, rather than standing in line at the grocery store or picking up dry cleaning. Having her help allowed me to keep going. This is how you secure your job success."

Titi also made certain that she worked in a pro-family environment, cultivating relationships with working mothers and with men whose partners were not stay-at-home parents.

"I wanted to work in a place where people talk about their families and where leaving early to get to their kids' baseball games was a nonevent."

Not only did she try to choose family-friendly cultures, but she led by example, talking openly about scheduling things like early departures for school plays or doctors' appointments to "normalize it for my teams."

Another key element for Titi was picking the right partner with whom to raise a family. "The most critical piece is whom you choose as your partner. The most important way for you to show up in the workplace and be competitive is by partnering with someone who is willing to be just as engaged with the kids and do their fair share at home. If I had to do all the childcare and all the household stuff, I couldn't have done what I did professionally. Make sure your partner is a cheerleader for your success, viewing your win as a team win. If you pick the wrong person, you'll end up holding yourself back and making endless sacrifices or being unhappy."

Of course, life happens. Even Agnes, who has cheerleaders both at home and at work, and complete agency in her career at IBM, has those moments: "Does it mean that every day, every minute of my life I'm 100% sure that I've made the right choice? When my job takes me away from my children, of course it hurts my heart. Can I sign a paper somewhere with my blood saying there might be a moment in my life when I look back and think oh, maybe I should not have taken that five-day business trip? I can't. It's a choice that I make without fully knowing how I will feel about it in hindsight. But at least it is a choice made based on the support that I find here, discussions with my husband, and understanding the kind of mother I want to be."

And the kind of leader. Call me biased, but I happen to believe that our experiences as parents enhance our ability to motivate, inspire, and care for the individuals who report to us, and beyond. As working moms, we also need to believe in ourselves and the legacy we are building for our families and as we blaze that trail to parity. This is not the time to be modest.

Which brings me back to Donna. She demonstrated resilience during Covid, one of the most harrowing periods in human history – the same inner strength that powered her through the personal trials of early motherhood. Her compassion for the millions of frontline workers when Covid first hit reminds me of some of the national and international leaders we referenced at the beginning of this book. She made their safety and well-being paramount, she pivoted quickly to the new reality, and she aligned resources and set policies that not only protected workers, but empowered them to get essential goods to communities around the world.

Donna was brand new to the role, yet she adapted. "All of a sudden I was in Arkansas with my bags, not knowing even where to go and realizing this was not going to be like any other job I've ever had."

When large corporations panicked and laid off hundreds of thousands of employees, Donna kept hiring – half a million new employees in three and a half months – making sure they had enough personnel to step in when existing associates went on paid emergency leave. The protective emergency Covid policies she established were becoming a blueprint for the rest of the retail world.

She was not just fearless, she was extremely effective. Now that's what I call the strength of a mother.

* * *

Your Path to the Top Checklist

Choose a career and workplace environment that fully supports your choices. If you find yourself in a culture that puts you in a penalty box for balancing work and life, it's not the right fit.

Stay in it, even when it's rough. Recognize that you don't always have to be sprinting at every inflection point of your career.

Some weeks you're crushing it; sometimes you're just hoping not to get crushed.

Be gracious to yourself and ditch perfectionism. Our society puts a lot of unrealistic expectations on women and what a "good mother" is. Give yourself some grace. You can be an awesome mother without making weekly excursions to the farmers' market to purchase organic vegetables to make your from-scratch baby food. Don't get caught up in scoring an A+ on everything or you'll be exhausted and resentful.

Trust that having a career ultimately sets the example for your children, regardless of gender. They may wish you were there 100% of the time, but when they are older, they'll be proud to call you their role model.

Develop a long-term plan, just as you would for the business or team that you are leading. Expect to pivot and adapt but stick to the overall vision to manifest the life and career you deserve.

Find your village. We all need other people around us to make our lives work. If you have children, invest in the best child care you can afford so you don't have to worry about your kids while you are at work. Figure out who, among your friends and family members, you can lean on when you need it – and be sure to give back to them in return when you have the capacity to do so.

Prioritize, then outsource to achieve what's most important to you. You work too hard during the week to deprive yourself of quality time with the family in the checkout line of Trader Joe's. Having it all doesn't mean doing it all.

Believe in yourself. Trust that the inner strength, compassion, multitasking, and decision-making as a parent has made you into the great leader you are today. You handled childbirth, breastfeeding, sleep training, remote learning, and teenage rebellion, after all.

CHAPTER 7

The Relationship Infrastructure

Do not follow where the path may lead. Go instead where there is no path and leave a trail.

—Muriel Strode (American poet)

Shards of broken glass ceilings surround Sarah Mensah.

In 2021, she became the first Black woman to hold Nike's vice president general manager role for North America, the sports retail giant's most important market. She was also the first Black woman to lead its Asia, Pacific, and Latin America operations. For almost two decades before joining Nike, Sarah worked her way up from corporate sales manager at the Portland Trail Blazers to become executive vice president and chief operating officer of the NBA franchise – one of the highest-ranking women executives in the testosterone-charged professional sports league. Sarah's leadership style is collaborative, empowering, and inspiring. It's her mission to bring other women forward, and she's well-known in the industry for mentoring and promoting diverse and underrepresented talent within her leadership team.

"I make it an active practice of saying to women: *You could lead this, you could be the one,*" Sarah told me. "It's so important for people to hear that. You shouldn't have to be a unicorn. I absolutely love to reinforce for all the brilliant women that I see and talk to regularly that they have that capability and could very well get there."

Sarah was echoing the passion for mentoring and coaching that drives so many of the great women leaders I met during the research for this book. Recognizing that success does not exist in a vacuum (and having been mentored themselves), they are constantly seeking innovative ways to pay it forward. Being the first and only woman leader wasn't acceptable to any of them. Rather, they wanted to become the latest of many, and they understood their role at this critical juncture in history to help more women leapfrog into leadership positions.

Women leaders like Sarah are stepping into their power and empowering others, through coaching, mentorship, sponsorship, affinity groups – intentional ways to build that talent pipeline and fix the leaks so that more women remain on the senior leadership path. Creating a network of internal and external allies is key to putting women on the succession radar because the usual methods of climbing up the corporate ranks often don't apply. We need to get noticed for our accomplishments without having to thump our chests, earning our recognition and place in the corporate hierarchy while still being true to ourselves. We need to seek our mentors, or "personal boards" from all walks of life and find opportunities to mentor in return. Not only does this approach help us to build dream teams among our direct reports, but it also seeds the talent pipeline, leaving the door open for the next generation of women to rise through the ranks. It takes a village to reach parity, because sometimes it's not enough to let the work speak for itself.

Mentoring and coaching women while forging a path that others can follow are essential to fixing the leaks – and lack of parity – in the leadership pipeline. Women need to be able to see themselves as leaders and mirror what that looks like to others. To bridge that chasm between where we are and where we need to be, we need to find the most impactful ways to elevate each other, building whole communities for women leaders both within our organizations and externally through industry forums, schools, and social media.

"I'm hoping that what I'm doing now will enable women to break through one ceiling, then another, then another,"

Sarah told me. "I want someone who could stand on my shoulders, shatter through the glass, and I want her to find someone to stand on hers, and so on, and so on. But we must find a way to do it at scale."

Sarah remembers all too well what it was like to be the only one. Growing up in Portland, Oregon, she was the only girl to train as a track athlete. The entire local track club was male. Every morning before practice, everyone warmed up by doing a two-mile lap around the playing field and, even though it wasn't a race, everyone sprinted towards the end of the warmup to have the fastest time. Sarah was determined not to let her physical differences put her behind, so she went harder and faster than everyone else and blew past their expectations.

"I started telling myself, *I am not going to be the last competitor. I am going to beat somebody!*"

Sarah brought that competitive muscle with her when she joined the NBA, with a deep understanding of how it felt to set the bar, train hard to win, and "more importantly, make a plan to get better."

That athletic upbringing, and familiarity with an all-male athletic environment, helped her to stand out and excel. Her talent as a business executive caught the attention of the legendary David Stern, who was then the NBA commissioner. Throughout her early career she felt encouraged, enabled, and "seen" by the late basketball icon, who had built the league into a global powerhouse and changed the conversation around HIV by embracing Earvin "Magic" Johnson Jr. at a time when the virus was most feared. With this male ally "showing up for me" early in her career, Sarah's confidence as a leader grew.

"I never felt from David that my being a woman, least of all a Black woman, was going to hold my career back in the NBA. I'm super-grateful that I had somebody like David who took a personal interest and let me know he believed in me."

That confidence built up over time, with Sarah at times struggling to "trust myself and believe that my insights and perspective matter." She told me, "There was no blueprint for how to extend my leadership and use my voice." When she joined Nike, another NBA star helped Sarah to instill that self-belief. Working on his brand, "I had the opportunity to sit at the table with Michael Jordan. I was able to learn and draft off of his example. I understood that all success requires us to stretch and push beyond our comfort zones. The intensity and inspiration of being challenged by the GOAT to achieve something more stays with me to this day."[1]

Open Door

Those early mentors and allies made a lasting impression on Sarah. But the lack of women at the top levels of leadership in sports had been burned into her brain. So, as she rose, she made a point to empower others. Her open-door leadership style is not just about including others in the conversation and receiving their input. It's about giving people the opportunity to take the reins in critical decision-making.

"As a leader, it's so important to create those spaces. I'm comfortable listening and allowing my team – many of whom are senior female leaders – to help with the solution. These are the future leaders at Nike, and they're coming up with a lot of the strategies that will define our future."[2]

Sarah also coaches the next generation of women leaders to speak up for their ideas, sharing stories about her own athletic past competing among men. "In business we are competing to win, so it's important that your ideas matter. Your innovative thoughts and plans need to be considered, so you've got to feel like you are enabled to put those forth. You can't just wait for someone to tell you it's okay to speak up."

It's not just the women on her executive team who are beneficiaries of this kind of advice. As Sarah has become a more prominent figure, she's been attracting large numbers of followers and fans through social media platforms like LinkedIn. She noticed that her reach extends beyond the company to women of all industries and stages in life. Black women and girls especially have messaged her, either to ask advice or simply to say how inspired they are to see themselves mirrored in a woman at the top. The more Sarah uses her voice, the larger her following, and the more she is using her power to influence, mentor, and affirm the choices and ambitions of other women at scale.

She's intentional, taking the time to answer texts and emails from women across different professions, including leaders of nonprofit organizations as well as businesses. She makes herself available, both internally at Nike and externally, offering encouragement, validating how they are feeling, listening to them vent their frustrations, or simply sharing her own thoughts and experiences.

"I've tried to prioritize those conversations and that has led to loose communities of similarly minded women who are interested in advancing their careers, their ideas, and their strategies."

When I interviewed Sarah in the summer of 2022, she was still feeling her way into this role as a leader of leaders, growing in self-awareness about the impact the power of her voice can have in these more expansive and public forums. It's a process, "because we're trained as women to be humble and to not really think about using our power overtly," she explained. But women leaders like Sarah are having a profound influence simply by being who they are and having other people see them and their successes.

"I'm just now learning that the more I speak authentically and openly about the challenges that I'm having and leading, the more I can have an impact on the cross-section of women who are experiencing those same challenges," Sarah told me.

In Her Shoes

My first step in exploring the executive search industry was to get an internship at one of the world's leading search firms and, within weeks, my decision to dedicate myself to this profession was cemented. I received offers to join several firms. I chose RRA's San Francisco office in large part because, as a woman who had a full-time working spouse and wanted to have children in the next few years, I would benefit from surrounding myself with success-ful women who had managed the simultaneous equation of work and family.

Liftoff comes more easily when you're in a place with role models: people you can look up to and ask for advice or even a little empathy on a tough day. This is not to say that men can't be helpful mentors – of course they can and will be – but there is nothing like having some-one who has walked a mile (or more) in your high heels.

Male Champions

Almost every successful woman leader I have spoken with had, in addition to inspiring women, a man in her life or career who saw something in her and helped her to see it in herself, whether it was a great boss or a loving and supportive father or husband. As Mesta CEO Marianne Bergmann Røren said about her dad, "He always told me and my two sisters, 'Girls, you can be anything.'" At the same time, Marianne credits her husband (who is also a

CEO at a company listed on the Norwegian Stock Exchange) for his continuous support. "He has always believed in me and has never put his own (impressive) career in front of mine," she said. "He's a thoroughly modern man who truly believes in diversity and takes full responsibility for his part at home and in the family."

Meanwhile, Susan Levine's father raised her to believe in herself. Susan, a long-tenured and highly trusted human capital partner at venerated Bain Capital, credits that early foundation with her ability to "tune out the noise" and drive with intensity towards her goals. Because of what her father taught her, she always understood that she was unique and capable of carving her own path.

"You can do whatever you set your mind to," he told her, and she took him at his word. He instilled in Susan a thirst for knowledge and an understanding that you can learn from anyone, regardless of gender, experience, or cultural background. In fact, the more diverse and different the individual, the greater the chance of learning something. That curiosity served Susan well at Bain, where she met Steve Barnes, managing director and head of Bain Capital's North American Private Equity business, who became one of her greatest mentors, investing proactively in her ongoing development, and Ken Hanau, a managing director and leader of Bain Capital Private Equity's North American Industrial Vertical, who today sits on the board of cleaning products company Diversey, Inc. with Susan.

Safe Zone

"I feel a psychological safety with Steve and Ken," Susan shared. "I always knew that if I was faced with a challenging situation or was having a hard time, I could reach out to either of them. I could ask them any question and they wouldn't judge me. In fact, just being able to have honest and open discussions with them would make me feel more confident. We all need people who back us and make us feel comfortable enough to ask them anything."

At each level of her career, gaining confidence was a process that took place in tandem with learning. The more experience Susan gained, the more "pattern recognition" enabled her to better analyze and predict outcomes. But that growth was underpinned by mentoring relationships, which helped guide and validate her decision-making, even as she entered the highest realms as a board executive.

These smart, successful women leaders were open-minded about whom to include in their networks. Sarah cultivated numerous male allies over the years, in part because of the nature of the business she is in.

"There were limited opportunities for women because they just didn't exist at that leadership level," Sarah recalled.

Her male allies and mentors include the Trail Blazers' general manager, Steve Patterson, who championed her throughout her NBA career. And Larry Miller, a former president of the Trail Blazers who became president of the Michael Jordan brand at Nike, recognized and promoted Sarah into her leadership roles (at the time of writing, he was chairman of the Jordan brand).

"As I talk to other women, I tell them it's possible to find men who are willing to play the role of mentor for you. It doesn't always have to be a woman in the exact same circumstances," said Sarah.

"Part of getting ourselves out of the current place we are in will require men to step up and play the role of real advocate, with a willingness to see beyond the historical stereotypes," Sarah told me.

Progressive male leaders and sponsors exist in all fields.

Julie Greenwald, Atlantic Records Group chairwoman and CEO introduced in Chapter 1, credits her first boss at the iconic hip-hop record label Island Def Jam, Lyor Cohen, with teaching her the fundamentals of business and leadership, and for being her sponsor, guide, and cheerleader at every critical juncture of her career. The outwardly gruff, cigar-chomping alpha male, who is now head of music at Google and YouTube, may not have seemed like the approachable type. But, as his personal assistant, then 22-year-old Julie had full access.

"Nothing was off limits to my eyes and ears," Julie told me. "I remember sitting on the makeshift couch in his office and soaking up all the information that was coming at him as a manager. He was just so open, honest, and direct, so I got to learn about the entire business very quickly."

Julie went on to run promotions at the record label, but Lyor's door was always open to her as they strategized the growth of the company together. As Island Def Jam went through major transitions, including an acquisition by Universal Group, Julie rose to executive vice president, gaining recognition through innovative marketing schemes that sold millions of albums. It was a turbulent time, "but not only was he generous with his time, he was transparent about what was going on in the company."

"Lyor signed me on as his partner at an early age, then put the battery on my back to help build Def Jam by offering me equity in the company."

Then, when Lyor left the label to run Warner Music's US operations, he took Julie with him, positioning her as president of Atlantic Records, which is owned by Warner Music Group, making her one of the few women in the music industry (at latest count, three) to head a label.

In the nearly two decades since, Julie has taken the same supportive and collaborative approach with her own leadership team, which has had a 50–50 gender split pretty much since she took the helm at Atlantic.

"Lyor made me feel like I was in it with him, as opposed to working for this organization that was not my own," Julie recalled. "He made me believe that Def Jam was my company too, and that I had the power to improve its performance.. . .That's the genius of him, and to this day I've tried to be the same way with my staff. I've always wanted everybody who worked at Atlantic Records to feel like they could put their handprints on the architecture of our company."

His Proudest Moment

When it was announced that Corie Barry would succeed Hubert Joly as CEO of Best Buy in April 2019, the markets weren't quite sure how to take the news. Hubert had been credited with a stunning turnaround of the business, and investors feared the company would its lose growth momentum with a new person at the helm. Corie, who had already been serving as the company's chief financial and strategic transformation officer, was deeply involved in that turnaround. Hubert, along with the retailer's board, chose her specifically because it would provide "leadership continuity." The board would remain "deeply involved" in the transition, with Hubert as executive chairman, keeping an office "literally right across the hall" from Corie to advise on matters like mergers, acquisitions, and external relationships. CEO successions, though critical to the long-term success of the business, are rarely so carefully orchestrated. But Hubert's process, which involved sponsoring and supporting a great woman leader, turned into what he described as "one of the things I'm proudest of in my career."

"It happened smoothly, without the company missing a beat," he wrote. "My successor Corie Barry was able to forge ahead, accelerate the company's growth strategy, and effectively deal with the pandemic – one of the most challenging, most multi-faceted [sic] crises the world has ever experienced – just nine months into her tenure."[3]

So yes, do tap men to be a part of your support network. There are many more of them in power than women, so their allyship can be invaluable. Besides, your coaches, mentors, and guides don't need to look like you. As we build out our infrastructure of relationships, diversity can be a huge advantage. We need a variety of professional, personal, casual, and formal relationships in multiple arenas.

Dual Network

For us to be able to get to where we need to be in terms of representation and parity, the traditional concept of networking is not enough. A 2019 *Harvard Business Review* study found that, because women seeking executive leadership positions often face cultural and political obstacles that men do not, they need broader and deeper contacts. The research, which analyzed social networks and job placement among MBA graduates based on 4.5 million anonymized email messages, found that men who had the most centrality – or were connected to multiple contact "hubs" – in the MBA student network were 1.5 times more likely to find jobs with the highest levels of responsibility and pay. Because that centrality helps with access to job market information, it was the critical factor in success even after accounting for undergraduate GPA, test scores, sociability, country of origin, and work experience. Yet for women, that centrality within the social network was not enough. To achieve the same success in job placement they also needed an inner circle of close female contacts, despite having similar qualifications to men.

This dual network is essential for women because this inner circle can provide a range of support and insights around potential challenges they might face. "This inner circle might provide information about whether a firm has equal advancement opportunities for men and women, or whether an interviewer might ask about plans to start a family and the best way to respond," writes Brian Uzzi, a professor at the Kellogg School of Management at Northwestern University and author of the study. Women who had the dual network landed jobs that were 2.5 times higher in authority and pay than women MBA graduates who did not, the study found.

But even a dual network isn't enough to fix the leaky pipes altogether. The Kellogg study suggests that women also need to be more strategic in the way they network. "First *seek quality over quantity* in your overall network," writes Uzzi. "Remember: centrality, in this context, is less a function of how many people you know but who those people are."

Starting higher within an organization, and advancing at the same pace as men, requires strategic networking with diverse individuals who are connected to multiple networks and "embracing randomness."

"The more you associate with similar-minded or experienced people, the less likely you will be to diversify your network and inner circle," Uzzi continues. Those who stick to workplace or industry affinity groups risk getting trapped in a closed inner circle, where people are too interconnected. They have the same or similar contacts, which limits opportunities. But, again, it's not just something a woman manager or executive should be expected to do entirely on her own. To help develop their female talent, employers should also create more diverse affinity groups across different functions. As Uzzi suggests, "Rather than creating just an affinity group of female coders, for example, populate a separate group with members from a cross-section of the organization that increase the chances of making unexpected connections, to better inform and support individuals."[4]

The Once-a-Month Rule

Jennifer Goldfarb, the co-founder of Ipsy whom you met in Chapter 3, exercises her networking muscle regularly, engaging with anyone and everyone who has achieved a level of success, regardless of whether they are in the same business or share a similar career path. While she was never enrolled in a formal mentoring program, she sought out individuals and engaged with them, turning them into mentors before they even realized what was happening. "I made them my mentors even if they didn't necessarily sign up for that role," Jen shared.

Jen was most drawn to those who were different from her because she recognized she could gain more complementary skill sets and insights from those she could develop organically than if she had just stayed within her own circle of business and social contacts. As a result, she has benefited from insights on a range of issues, from how to navigate a particular path in business to how to juggle being a mother with a demanding, high-performance career. "I was able to gather a lot of tidbits from many, many women along my path who were so influential to me."

As we were talking, it occurred to me that some women, lacking the social confidence or connections, may wonder how to reach out and engage with someone they admire. It's not easy for everyone to cold-call a stranger, for example. But the more you do it, the easier it gets. "I have never had a senior, more accomplished woman say no to me," Jen shared.

Whether via LinkedIn messaging, email, picking up the phone, or approaching someone in-person at a business or social event, having a clear reason why you are asking to make that connection helps. One opener might be: *Hi, my name is _____ and I wanted to introduce myself because I really admire how you accomplished _____. I am currently in the process of_____ and would love to know your thoughts about how I could navigate this situation.*

"If you have the courage and take the initiative, most people are flattered to be asked. And a little bit of humility combined with a little bit of honesty about what you hope to derive from the relationship goes a long way," Jen shared.

Jen wasn't always so proactive as a networker. As a young mother with a demanding career, she had made the conscious decision to keep her head down, stay in her lane, and work hard at her job, but spend the rest of her precious free time with her family, as so many women do. If you're a young mother, it's understandable that you would prioritize doing your best work in the office, then come home immediately every day to be the most attentive and caring parent possible, to the exclusion of almost everything else. But after a few years triaging her daily duties this way, Jen found herself at a serious career disadvantage.

She hit a point where she no longer felt fulfilled in her career. She was bored and eager for a new challenge. But her "dual track" focus on job and family meant she'd lost sight of people in her periphery, and she had no contacts outside of the company where she'd been working all those years.

"That was a huge lightbulb moment," Jen told me. "I found myself without a lot of options because I had not been building relationships more broadly, beyond my company."

To "fix the mistake," Jen set herself the goal of doing at least one networking activity a month. She committed and carved out that time, however hectic her life got. It didn't necessarily have to be a formal business event. Grabbing a coffee with a mentor, going for a walk with a former colleague, attending a class or conference, or participating in an industry-oriented dinner or cocktail party – all count as networking interactions. Of course, you need to be strategic about what activities you say "yes" to – because you likely can't do them all. But taking just one day a month to invest back in yourself will likely reap significant rewards, both tangible and intangible.

"It was super-valuable, because if you're doing that 12 times a year, you are out in the mix," said Jen.

At first, she thought of networking as "kind of cheesy, like you're in it for yourself." But the benefits turned out to be plentiful, often unexpected, and surprisingly not so self-serving. Growing her network enabled Jen to hire and promote others just as much as they could help accelerate her career path. She reframed her thinking and came to see networking as "a strategic investment." It didn't just reward her with the contacts that she needed to evolve from investment banker to beauty industry entrepreneur, but also with a pool of highly talented and passionate individuals she could tap to help her to found and grow her own company.

A Business of One's Own

As Jen demonstrated, becoming an entrepreneur is another bold way to accelerate your career and the journey to parity. When you start a business of your own, you get to build your own corporate culture – one that gives women full and equal access to opportunities. Entrepreneurs get to be sponsors at scale, designing their organizations to be supportive of women at all stages of their careers.

"When you are your own boss, you can leapfrog over so many of the problems that women face when they're stuck in a big organization, whether it's not getting fair pay or being passed over for promotions," Jen explained. "All that goes away if you're your own boss. Not only can you control your own destiny, but you can really set the kind of culture, values, and belief systems that you want your whole organization to benefit from."

Jen didn't start out as an entrepreneur. She first worked as an investment banker. But she'd seen enough of that world to realize she wanted to be an operator and build something "from the inside." So she switched careers, joining the executive leadership team of the beauty company Bare Escentuals and learning about the industry before co-founding Ipsy.

Jen learned how to do what she loved by networking and navigating business environments from New York City to Silicon Valley, as well as through her MBA at Stanford Business School, where "entrepreneurism was at the heart of everything." Exposing herself to different people and ecosystems planted the seed and connected her with people in the investment community who could help her to grow her idea into a beauty industry disruptor.

"I didn't always think I was going to be an entrepreneur," Jen shared. "But I learned over time that I like to start when things are small, evolving them into something from nothing."

Not only did founding a business scratch that entrepreneurial itch, but it empowered her to empower others. By being the boss, she could have a direct impact on their career trajectories and experiences in the workplace. She could set the rules, personally ensuring that the women who work for her could enjoy a family-friendly environment with both flexibility and opportunities for professional development.

"There's so much value in women being leaders of companies, and not just on the founding team, but founders or co-founders."

Women founding and owning businesses gets us faster to 50–50 in terms of both leadership positions and wealth creation, because we have more equity when we are there from the beginning, which too often has not been the case with older businesses established by men. Sadly, a shockingly paltry 2% of venture capital in 2021 in the United States went to female-founded companies,[5] further deepening the chasm of wealth that exists between the genders. This needs to change to help accelerate our path to financial parity and freedom.

"It's structurally essential for the economy to get to 50–50, and women starting companies allows for bigger and faster societal change," Jen observed. "You're not just working your way up through an organization and impacting your career and the careers of your team. Coming in and running things from the top makes a difference to a much broader group of people, from the entire company you started to the other businesses that you are interfacing with. So the more women who run businesses, the more exponential impact we can have on the world."

Board Benefits

More women at the very top of any organization, start-up or otherwise, will also help to fix the talent pipeline leaks and help women at scale. There is movement in various markets to require more gender-balanced representation on corporate boards, with the Nasdaq announcing in August 2021 that it requires any company that lists on their exchange to have at least two diverse members, including at least one woman. The European Union has gone much further, with a deal among its member nations to ensure that at least 40% of board seats go to the "underrepresented sex" (i.e. women).

Even without these requirements, it is in the obvious economic interests of companies to have more women on boards because countless studies demonstrate that companies with more diversity perform better financially. Businesses with three or more women on boards had a five-year earnings per share growth of 37% versus –0.8% for companies with no women on boards, according to MSCI ESG research 2016 – an independent provider of ESG data and ratings related to corporate responsibility.[6] A 2016 Credit Suisse report[7] found boards with at least one woman resulted in a 3.5 percentage point increase in excess compound returns per year, higher valuations, and superior stock price performance. A more recent March 2020 study by Bankwest Curtin Economics Centre in Australia found that a 10% increase in women on boards resulted in a 4.9% increase in corporate market value.[8]

Besides improved financial performance and fewer controversies related to governance, the study also found that board-level parity led to the "recruitment and retention of talented women employees who respect companies with women in executive and board leadership."[9] In other words, having women on your board results in other women being able to "see it to be it."

So having more women visible at the highest level of the relationship infrastructure is one of the most impactful forms of mentorship. Simply by being who they are, and where they are, these senior executives can influence the lives of the next generation. They can hold up a mirror to high-profile leaders like Sarah Mensah, who teach their strategies in business and life by being open, accessible, and true to themselves. As Sarah put it, "Seeing another woman have success, that is one of the most powerful forms of mentorship there is."

* * *

Your Path to the Top Checklist

Reinforce their power. Let potential women leaders know that they belong in those higher positions. They shouldn't have to rely on their own inner strength. They need to hear that they can get there themselves.

Be the latest of many. It's better than the first and only. Success does not exist in a vacuum, and great women leaders recognize they must seek innovative ways to pay it forward. They have a critical role to play in helping women leapfrog to leadership positions.

Build broad networks of contacts. Women seeking executive leadership positions often face cultural and political obstacles men do not, so they need a deeper and more expansive network of relationships. If you ever find yourself in a career rut, learn you're not being paid fairly, or want to get onto a board, having an anemic network will not serve you well.

Cultivate male allies. Mentors don't always have to look like you. We also need men as sponsors because there are still too few women at senior leadership levels. We need all the support we can get, so don't discriminate – cultivate!

Avoid sameness. As we build out our infrastructure of relationships, diversity can be a huge advantage. We need a variety of professional, personal, casual, and formal relationships in multiple arenas. Too much similarity results in overlapping contacts and limits opportunities.

Create multiple affinity groups. To help develop their female talent, employers should also create more diverse affinity groups across different functions. Populate groups with members from a cross-section of the organization to increase the chances of making unexpected connections.

Just ask. When you identify a potential mentor, be bold and take the initiative; most leaders are flattered to be asked. Then figure out a clear reason why you are contacting them and be transparent about it.

Elevate through entrepreneurship. Business founders can be sponsors at scale, designing their organizations to be supportive of women at all stages of their careers. Shaping women leaders and enabling them to develop their careers in lockstep with a growing business is good for everyone.

Balance the board. More women at the very top, including corporate boards, will also help to fix the talent pipeline leaks and help more women at a faster pace. Research has shown that "see it to be it" at the board level has profound and concrete benefits that do not just get us closer to parity but also enrich the business.

Mentor at scale. It's possible to inspire others and mentor by example. Mirror what's possible to others, then be open and accessible through social media forums. The more women leaders speak authentically and openly about the challenges they face, the greater the impact they can have on the cross-section of women who are experiencing those same challenges.

CHAPTER 8

The Long Tail

We must have perseverance and above all confidence in ourselves. We must believe that we are gifted for something, and that this thing must be attained.

—Marie Curie, chemist and physicist

Just weeks into her move from Singapore to London, England, where her husband had been transferred, Ng "Gim" Choo was already getting bored with her new life. As is often the case when your partner gets a job relocation, Gim had set aside her thriving career as an auditor at EY to keep the family together. Although she was on a senior management track, the move forced her to make a difficult choice. Her son and daughter were just two and four years old, so the idea of one parent flying back and forth from London to Singapore and becoming what's known in that part of the world as an "astronaut" was unacceptable to her. Instead, she settled into expat life, practicing her English with more regularity, taking flower arranging classes, and grabbing lunch with old colleagues when they were passing through town.

"I really missed the corporate world and all the office chatter," Gim recalled. "I wanted to be a part of something bigger again."

After a few months, Gim decided to throw herself into her children's education and she stepped up to become a parent volunteer at her daughter's school. She was intrigued by the British education system because it was completely different from anything she'd experienced back home. In Singapore, her daughter, E-Ching, who was academically gifted and today is a linguist, had not enjoyed going to school. Teachers were strict and children were instructed according to rigid formats and rote memorization.

"That traditional model in Singapore 30 years ago was like a pressure cooker," Gim explained. "Sometimes we bully our children to learn, and when they don't do it the way we expect, we punish them. But you don't learn by fear."

When she first moved to the United Kingdom, Gim admits she was concerned about how her daughter would adapt to a different culture. But at her new private preschool in London, E-Ching was thriving. Each morning she didn't have to be told to brush her hair and put on her crisp uniform. She was always ready and at the door, her colored pencils neatly organized in her knapsack. The little girl was even disappointed that there was no school on weekends. Gim just had to find out what was different about the English school system. What made it so stimulating? So she sat in on classes, talked to the teachers, got to know the other students, and soaked up all the information she could about the teaching style and curriculum, where children were respected and their interests celebrated. She was motivated to start a similar school when she went back to Singapore, a school where children were respected and their creativity and personality were nurtured.

When the family returned to Singapore, Gim sprang into action. She talked to other parents, assessed the market and in 1995, founded her first school, called EtonHouse. It was a disaster. Parents were skeptical about a curriculum where children were having "too much fun" and didn't have to do homework because they couldn't grasp this foreign concept of inquiry-based learning. She also had to convince the educators to offer a bilingual education for children as young as 18 months, something they were not familiar with in those days. Gim lost $1 million that first year alone. Naysayers told her this wouldn't work in the context of Singapore.

"You were an auditor. What do you know about education?" someone asked her.

Yet she knew that in Singapore the current system wasn't working. "Rote learning and memorization will not help children in the long run to be competent or successful because these are not transferable skills," she told them.

Hands On

Gim spent a lot of time educating the parents and advocating for a pedagogy that was focused on the children's competencies and interests, not the teachers' wants. Those first few years were grueling, and not just because she was trying to start a one-woman education revolution. Gim herself was in the process of learning. Humble enough to put herself in the place of the teachers she hired, Gim got her preschool teacher training certificate and a master's degree in educational management because "I had to understand what happens inside a classroom." That meant getting her hands in the chalk dust and teaching the children herself, which was an eye-opener.

"One day after a long day at work I was exhausted. My clothes were messy with all the classroom activities. I was wearing a red skirt with buttons going all the way down the side and, by the end of the day, all the buttons were gone," Gim recalled with a chuckle. "With children that age you have to be all things: teacher, caregiver, entertainer, even the police!"

Realizing exactly how much energy went into the job, she decided to increase the annual leave for teachers to 35 days, compared to the industry practice of 21 days. Gim has such an abiding respect for educators that she has since founded several free professional development programs for teachers at all schools in the region, not just at EtonHouse, to help attract and retain more talent.

"Children first, teachers second, and shareholders third," Gim told me, although, make no mistake, she added, EtonHouse has always been run like a business. She attributes her entrepreneurial skills to her Chinese immigrant grandmother, who built a successful sesame oil business. But her "four Ps" – "Passion, Perseverance, People, and Professional Development" – do not include "profit," despite the fact that she built her career crunching numbers. "When you do something with passion and establish your reputation, the operating surplus will follow," she explained.

By her second and third years as a school founder, word started to spread about the bright, natural young leaders coming out of her school and excelling in the next phase of their education. Popular demand and word of mouth led her to open several preschools and eventually primary schools, then middle school, and high school. By the time we spoke in September 2022, two days after her 70th birthday, this mother of three and grandmother of three had established an education empire, with 120 campuses ranging from preschool to high school in Singapore, in 11 countries in the region – including Vietnam, Malaysia, Indonesia, and Japan – as well as several campuses in China.

Today it is widely accepted that inquiry-based learning is the best way for children to learn. The groundbreaking education brand boasts long waiting lists, with eager parents vying to get their children into this institution with a reputation for nurturing independent, self-starting and academically accomplished graduates who go on to the world's top colleges, earning Gim a top 20 spot as one of *Forbes'* 2021 Asia Power Businesswomen.[1]

Gim's true career calling happened later in life, after she had raised her kids and stepped out of the corporate world for more than a decade. Knowing all too well how hard it has been for many women at that point in their lives to get back in the game, much less become an industry powerhouse, I was curious to find out Gim's mindset when she took those bold steps.

"It's one thing to find a great school for your child and volunteer as a parent; it's quite another to start one yourself. How did you find that drive?" I asked her.

"I think of my life as a series of chapters," Gim answered. "Auditing was the first, being a mother was the second, founding this school was the third. And this book is still being written."

A Different Timeline

Gim exemplifies what I call "the long tail" possessed by many women who, with their extended life expectancy, resilience, perseverance, and adaptability, have reinvented themselves and their careers to be relevant, vibrant, and successful well into their 70s and 80s. For them, the age for "midcareer" is 55, not 35, because it is around that age they start to ascend, whether in the same profession or industry in which they began, or some entirely new venture. For these leaders, age and experience are powerful assets and not something to be sidelined or shelved.

To my point, Gim was about to embark on her doctorate degree in education at the time we spoke. She expects to complete her doctorate in education EdD by the age of 75.

Research has shown that women can work harder and longer than men. According to the workplace productivity platform Hive,[2] which in 2018 anonymously sourced information from more than 3,000 working men and women, women work 10% harder than men at the office. Not only do we live longer, but we have the energy and endurance to be productive and inspiring leaders well into that phase of life where most men choose to retire and hit the links. While conscious and unconscious biases and ageism often put women "out to pasture" as they are reaching menopause or beyond, this is the time when their children have left the nest, and they finally have the bandwidth to reach new levels as leaders. As Gim put it, "It is never too late to pursue your dreams. Age should not be a deterrent. Nor should the hiatus from work to raise your children."

Grace Period

The experience of researching this book has made me realize that one of the things I would have once said women need to do – get on the fast track to career success at an early age before having children – may no longer be necessary. Instead of thinking about careers in terms of a ladder to climb, I now prefer the analogy of a web to be traversed, giving women the latitude to take a not-so-straight line through the corporate rungs. Webs are strong yet elastic, comprised of thousands of tiny strands coming together from multiple directions, and sticky enough to capture and retain a woman at every juncture of her career. We are living longer, so we don't all have to reach the zenith of our careers by the age of 50.

The arc of a typical career has been created by men for men, and it follows a timeline of going "all in" on careers in their 30s – the same period in life when many women may also be focused on other things and missing out on those peak earning years.

Leaders need to view the totality of a woman's career through a whole new lens. The traditional orthodoxy surrounding careers and the pressure to "make it" by our 30s must shift. Organizations need to be more open-minded to bending or extending what we have typically thought of as the successful career trajectory – which, let's face it, really benefits men, who often don't take the same amount of family leave as women, at least not yet. Similarly, DE&I policies must take into account ageism, even including accommodations for employees going through menopause, as an increasing number of progressive companies in Europe are already doing.

As a leadership advisor, I've seen ageism and bias toward people who have not "made it" by a certain age, but as we continue to evolve as a species (currently, most people born in 2020 or later will live to be over 100 years old, according to best estimates), our norms about what success looks like also need to change and adapt. Women currently comprise 83% of centenarians, while men only make up 17% of that population. It's why organizations need to give people – but especially women – the grace to slow down at certain points in their careers, and to power up again when they are ready.

It doesn't always have to be a sprint. There are moments in our careers when it makes sense to busily plant seeds. But there are also times when we need to relax a bit and harvest. Why not build in career chapters, taking a break and going from the career marathon to merely walking the course for a year or two? Or try some lateral moves within your organization to expand and grow without running out of breath.

Amy Bunszel, whom you met in Chapter 1, is a rare and impressive trailblazer in the tech world. As the EVP of Architecture, Engineering, and Construction (AEC) Design at software industry leader Autodesk, Amy had a fresh take on the stale notion of a career ascent. When you are considering making a job change, investigate the possibilities in your current organization. I am not suggesting there aren't moments when it makes sense to leave, but don't be too hasty. Assuming you like the company culture, and it already feels like a fit, even if you want to do something wildly different from what you are currently doing (e.g. moving from finance to sales), chances are that if there is any possibility of making such a move, your current employer will give you a shot at something even a few standard deviations away from your current role. It's another spider's web approach to building a career that sticks.

By sometimes choosing to move *across* the organization instead of up, you can harvest all that you've already built in terms of experience and relationships without having to go through a more drastic move. It may also be a way to build the essential skill sets that qualify leaders to become CEO, and that too many women miss out on, like operations or P&L experience, for example. According to RRA's most recent research, only 20% of P&L leaders are women.[3]

Take a breath and press pause to take stock of where you are, and where you need to go. Slow down to see the path ahead more clearly. As Amy put it, "Not all of life has to be a race. We don't only have to have one speed to be successful."

Take Two

Organizations need to do more to help their employees find that breathing space. Enabling us to dial it up or dial it down and make it more socially acceptable to slow the pace at times helps everyone from new parents to elderly caregivers to individuals simply looking to explore another side of themselves.

Bain & Company had this in mind when they implemented flexible working options to adjust your pace – including the ability to work part time or Take a Break. Take a Break (popularly known as "Take Two") is a program that allows consultants at any level to take a multi-month "mini-sabbatical" for any reason.

"We made it easy and safe to do so," explained Heidi Locke Simon, the former Bain partner you met in Chapter 1. "You didn't have to have a nervous breakdown or a death in the family. You just had to plan ahead and let HR know."

That timeout and ability to "get into a different rhythm" helped them to come back more energized. Not everyone took advantage, but just knowing it was an option boosted loyalty and morale. Those who did avail themselves of the program often came back to new and better assignments, so no one felt they would be stigmatized if they wanted to take a summer off, for example.

"And people did the most interesting things, like a silent meditative retreat, an extended honeymoon, exploring a new business idea, or traveling around the globe," Heidi recalled. "And they came back feeling like they could conquer the world."

This kind of flexibility has big benefits. Corporations currently spend billions on recruitment and retention, so why not do all they can to preserve this invaluable employee base? Given the severe shortage of experience and talent in the workforce, it behooves them to step back and view their talent development in terms of decades. Employers can no longer afford to focus solely on the under-50s when the global population is aging as the talent pool is shrinking. Longer-term planning and creating opportunities for people of all ages will help to recruit the best leaders and engender greater loyalty. And companies that focus on recapturing boomeranging colleagues returning from a leave, even offering retraining in some cases, can yield significant benefits. Failure to shift to a more holistic view of a woman's life and career is a missed opportunity to benefit from her skills and wisdom as she hits her true prime.

A Shrinking Pool

Economists in the US predict the declining labor force participation rate is going to blunt economic growth as the working age population of 15- to 64-year-olds declines to historic lows.[4] The same thing is happening around the world. In Japan, that same demographic is expected to decline from 87 million in 1995 to 69 million by 2030.[5]

Meanwhile, 25% of workers in the US and UK are predicted to be over 55 by 2025 and "this same cohort of workers is the fastest growing in every country"[6] – a trend fueled by the fact that Baby Boomers are retiring at a rate faster than Millennials can replace them. It's why, in Australia, where the unemployment rate has hit a 48-year low with the second tightest labor market in the world, 60 is becoming the new 40.

In Their Prime

Examples abound of female leaders who are crushing it well into their 60s as executives, or through a midcareer switch as entrepreneurs, philanthropists, or academics. It's almost as if, by the time men start cashing their pension checks, women are revving up for the next phase.

Perhaps the longest tail belonged to the late Queen Elizabeth II, who never rested during her 70-year reign. As I write this, watching the procession of her coffin to Westminster Abbey, I'm reminded of the 96-year-old's final days, when she somehow mustered the energy to swear in Liz Truss, the new prime minister of Britain – the Queen's 15th, no less. Rumor has it that courtiers tried to convince the frail monarch to sit that one out and let her son take care of it, but she insisted, telling them, "Of course I have to. It's my job."

She looked bright as she stood up to receive the politician, and her eyes had that usual sparkle, even though she was holding herself up with a cane. There was no way the longest-reigning monarch would have missed an opportunity to serve unless it was physically impossible for her to do so.

Nancy Pelosi, another long-reigning public figure and arguably one of the most powerful political figures alive today, is still serving as United States Speaker of the House at 81 years young. She didn't run for office until she was 47 and became the first female speaker at 66. Whatever your politics, we can all recognize that her energy and endurance are remarkable. It's why, when *Forbes* inaugurated its first "50 Over 50" list of great women leaders in 2021, aptly subtitled "Women Proving Success Has No Age Limit," the politician was prominently featured.

"People make their own decisions about their timing, and they don't have to comply with somebody else's view of how that should be," she told the magazine.[7] "It's about what works for them."

When *Forbes* first announced the new list, it was flooded with more than 10,000 nominations, suggesting that older accomplished women leaders, while virtually invisible in the media until then, are most definitely a thing. These individuals are outstanding leaders in multiple realms, from business to nonprofits to sports to science to academia. Among them were Cathie Wood, the founder of Ark Investment, 65, a pioneering figure on Wall Street whose firm's success is based on disruptive innovation, and Amy Adams Strunk, 66, the billionaire owner of the Tennessee Titans and one of a growing number of women who own NFL teams.

I was particularly struck by the story of Julie Wainwright. As the CEO of Pets.com, she was forced to shut the company down when the dot-com bubble burst in November 2000 (on the very day her husband asked for a divorce). But the e-commerce entrepreneur, now 65, picked herself up and went on to establish the RealReal, an online luxury consignment retailer worth more than $100 million. Looking back at the months following her public and personal crises, she remembers thinking, "Clearly, I'm not going to be able to get my dream job from someone else. I'm going to have to create my own."

Older women have long faced the double-barreled biases of ageism and sexism, yet these examples of resilience and entre-preneurism prove that there is not a finite window for success. The only thing that should be retired is the offensive phrase "past her prime." I think she might just be getting started.

Better Than Ever

Outside the US, there are countless other inspiring women lead-ers whose achievements only accelerated with age and who are crushing it in fields ranging from business to entertainment to the environment.

In Japan, Keiko Erikawa, 73, co-founded Koei Tecmo – one of the country's largest video game developers, worth $8.5 billion – and manages its $1.1 billion in assets. Erikawa, who along with Gim was recognized by *Forbes* as an Asian business power woman, became an outside director – and the only woman on the board – of investment company Soft-Bank Group. Other examples include Dame Sarah Gilbert, 58, the UK-based scientist who developed the AstraZeneca Covid vaccine, and Lady Amanda Fielding, 79, who founded the Beckley Foundation to research the health benefits of psychoactive substances and has co-authored more than 50 reports on the subject, including a groundbreaking brain imaging study about LSD.

In recent years, British television personality Anne Robinson, 76, was made the host of the hit game show *Countdown*. Jo Ruxton, 66, founder of Ocean Generation, was recognized by Queen Elizabeth II for her work on marine conservation and raising awareness about plastic waste in the oceans. And Anne Boden, 62, founded Starling Bank to help women entrepreneurs.

In 2020, at 52, Dame Sharon White, a former civil servant, became the first female chair of the John Lewis Partnership, one of the largest retailers in the UK, and was named Dame Commander of the Order of the British Empire for public service. She was also named one of *Fortune* magazine's "Most Powerful International Women" in 2020 and 2021. Asked by *Red* magazine what advice she would give to older women who feel their careers may be waning, Dame Sharon answered, "Your 50s is the time of life when you're more confident – you know yourself, what matters to you and what you are good at."[8]

Even those who have switched careers have developed strengths that can serve them well in a new endeavor. "I've found that skills developed in my 20s, 30s, and 40s in a different sector are transferable because the values behind what I have done have been consistent," Dame Sharon said.

Career expiration dates are so last century. Many of the above-mentioned leaders are highly visible, which is a good thing because, again, you really need to see it to be it. The more that women in the earlier stages of their careers can be exposed to energetic women of all ages being innovators, pioneers, trailblazers, and tycoons, the more they will see that the possible trajectory of their professional lives is limitless.

Out of the Shadows

It has never been more necessary to celebrate these women, because they represent a demographic that's often being pushed into the shadows yet again. Before Covid, women over 50 were on the way to becoming more of a force in the workplace, According to an April 2021 report by the Resolution Foundation,[9] a UK-based think-tank on employment and living standards, the employment rate for 50- to 64-year-olds hit 73% in 2019 – its highest point since the UK began comparing comparable data in 1975. Yet between the fourth quarters of 2019 and 2020 – when the global pandemic was in full swing – the employment rate for 50- to 69-year-olds (both men and women) shrank by 1.4 percentage points, compared to a 0.7% drop for 25- to 49-year-olds. For this group, particularly women, the pandemic furloughs hit hard, turning into a kind of forced early retirement.

Women already retire earlier than men because they tend to be about two years younger than their male partners, and many couples choose to retire at the same time. Because women's careers already exist on an artificially constrained timeline, with prime earning years lost for many who choose to raise a family, this curtailment, combined with the "pink tax" of earning less money on the dollar than men, hits us hard in terms of lifetime earnings and puts more women in financial peril in their later years.

But these foreshortened careers are also bad for companies, and their pipeline of next-generation leaders. A *Harvard Business Review* study that surveyed around 10,000 companies found that, despite ageism and false assumptions that older workers have less energy than their younger colleagues, they bring added value, with deep social networks and specific skill sets, experience, and wisdom they can share with their teams. A key takeaway of the research was that age should be added to companies' DE&I programs because, beyond the diversity of perspectives that feeds innovation, older workers create a sense of "psychological safety" in the workplace, bringing wisdom and calm that can help foster greater productivity.

"Many older people have learned not to get needlessly ruffled by the setbacks, internal politics, budget constraints, and limited resource allocation common in the world of work," notes *Forbes* columnist Aliza Knox.[10] "Younger people, still trying to prove themselves, are less experienced at assessing the lasting impact of today's obstacles, may take challenges personally, react emotionally, and fret unnecessarily about typical office hurdles. Older people can bring much needed equanimity to the office, ratcheting down the drama and serving as good role models of stamina and calm competence."

Raring to Go

One tool companies can consider is a "returnship" program, which offers skills training – essentially an internship – to those who have taken time off from work. Often the beneficiaries are women who are "trailing spouses," with partners in the military or a corporation who were relocated. These return-to-work programs can ensure more women can step back in after a hiatus, so that their naturally long tails don't get cut short. Cognizant, for example, an IT services multinational based in New Jersey, sponsors a 12-week paid "experience" for technology professionals who have been out of the workforce for at least two years. The company will then consider supporting someone who has gone through the program for any open positions.

"We believe a pause in your career to pursue other important life callings helps you emerge not only stronger, but raring to go," Cognizant says on its website.[11]

Value Added

Notably, many of the women chosen for the *Forbes* "50 Over 50" list were nominated by younger women they had mentored. It's that desire to pay it forward that drives seasoned top executives like Mindy Grossman to keep taking on new career challenges, attaining new heights of achievement even beyond the C-suite. "I figure I've been through enough crises, enough changes across enough industries that, you know, if I can add the value, that's fantastic," Mindy told me.

Mindy, 65, who most recently served as CEO of WW International, reinvigorating the company into a global wellness brand, has been dubbed the "turnaround queen" by famed journalist and fellow 60-something powerhouse Tina Brown. Mindy has been ranked among *Forbes'* 100 most powerful women in the world multiple times, was number 22 in *Fortune* magazine's "Top People in Business" list in 2014 and made the *Financial Times* top 50 women in world business in 2010 and 2011. She has served on the senior leadership team at Fortune 500 companies for decades, including Ralph Lauren, Tommy Hilfiger, and Nike, and a three-time CEO – of the Home Shopping Network and its former parent, IAC Retail, before WW.

Throughout her career, Mindy has been fearless in her choices. She once left without another job to go to after taking a principled stand. She joined a fashion company and took over its retail portfolio, having never been in retail. She joined Nike without a sports background. She leapt into television with no media experience.

"I've never been truly ready for any job I've ever taken," she told me. "I've never had the entire list of competencies."

Mindy also relishes the challenge of fixing a broken business that no one in the industry thought could be saved. In fact, she defies the so-called "glass cliff" phenomenon, where women are appointed to lead struggling companies and expected to fail. If anything, she runs towards that edge to prove what can be done.

"People think I'm insane for some of the roles I've taken," Mindy told me. "But I have always taken a lot of the risks that many people would not have taken because I believe that not taking the risk, is, in many cases, ultimately riskier."

Consummate Disruptors

As one of a handful of women running menswear companies, Mindy grew Ralph Lauren's Chaps division from $20 million to $250 million in three years. At HSN, which had eight CEOs cycle through in 10 years, she drastically revamped the business model with a series of bold moves, transforming it from a home shopping channel to a multiplatform business that leveraged consumers' shift to online and became a leader in digital retail. As she explained, "If you don't disrupt yourself, someone else will come along and disrupt you."

Mindy cleaned house at the flailing business, restructuring and redeploying assets. She even replaced all the old office chairs with state-of-the-art, ergonomic seats – symbolizing that it was a new era where the team would be positioned and supported for a new level of success. Mindy also took the company public in 2008, right before the global markets crashed. But by then she'd rebuilt the fundamentals of the business so that it could survive the crisis. She quickly pivoted HSN from selling luxury items to cookware and gadgets that could help households save money, befitting the mood of its customers in that moment.

"It was one of the toughest leadership times I ever had, because I knew I had the fate of 6,000 people and their families at stake,"[12] Mindy recalled, though she successfully guided the company through its recovery and continued growth.

Never one to turn down a challenge, and in fact restless for the next one, Mindy took over the leadership of what was then Weight Watchers – a sleepy legacy brand that had been losing members for years before Mindy took over in 2017. When she revamped it into WW International, she got Oprah Winfrey to join the board and built an entire digital community around the refreshed concept, which attracted 4.2 million subscribers by the time Mindy left the company at the end of 2021.

When Mindy and I spoke in the summer of 2022 there had been a lot of buzz about her next move. "Would you ever retire?" I ventured to ask.

"I hate that word," Mindy replied, adding, "I'm kidding!"

But not really. She decided to bring her considerable experience and expertise to the newly formed advisory and investment firm, Consello, which has an impressive partner roster including Tom Brady. Rather than run just one company, Mindy chose to work with CEOs and teams across a diverse portfolio of businesses. She is a partner at the firm and is also the Chairman of Consello Growth, a business development accelerator to unlock opportunities, create new revenue pipelines and transform existing businesses. She continues to serve on boards and is also focused on her personal investments, identifying visionary founders, many of whom are women and helping them in their entrepreneurial endeavors.

"I want to have impact. I want to take my knowledge and experience and utilize it in a way that is going to be beneficial, to support young people in that journey. That's where I get my energy. Helping make others successful has been the premise of my entire career."

Mindy, like Gim, calls it her next chapter, which also includes more philanthropic work like serving on the board of visitors of Columbia School of Engineering, where she is pushing for gender parity in the academics, and serving on the board and executive committee of UNICEF USA.

What also drives Mindy, and other long-tailed success stories like her, is an "insatiable curiosity" about what's next in her industry, or industries, and the best practices for leading and empowering others to new heights of success.

For EtonHouse's Ng Gim Choo, that mindset is necessary for the ultimate survival of the legacy she has built. "Always have an innovative mindset. . . .The world is changing so fast, so it is critical to keep up and continuously innovate and disrupt to stay relevant. We always have to look out for innovative ways to address the context of our families."[13]

While still involved in strategic and financial planning, Gim is transitioning the day-to-day operations of her business to her son while she focuses more of her attention on her company's charity division, the EtonHouse Community Fund, which aims to make quality education accessible to every child in Singapore.

"As we are in the education space we feel that we should share programs that EtonHouse has developed for underprivileged children," said Gim.

She still enjoys flower arranging, indulges her passion for Chinese calligraphy, and sets aside more time for her grandchildren, who are now in an EtonHouse school. But don't confuse this with slowing down.

"My life must have a purpose," Gim told me. "If I don't have that, I lose my reason to keep going. So I will work until I am too weak to get out of bed. Maybe then I will stop."

* * *

Your Path to the Top Checklist

Appreciate the value added. Age and experience are powerful assets and not something to be sidelined or shelved. Conscious and unconscious biases and ageism often put women "out to pasture," yet this is the time when their children have left the nest and they finally have the bandwidth to reach new levels as leaders.

Recalibrate the timeline. Leaders should view the totality of a woman's career through a whole new lens. Organizations need to give women the grace to slow down at certain points in their lives, and power up again when they are ready. Longer-term planning and creating opportunities for women at all ages will help to recruit the best leaders and engender greater loyalty.

Replace the ladder with a web. Give women the latitude to take a not-so-straight line through the corporate rungs. Webs are strong yet elastic, made up of thousands of tiny strands coming together from multiple directions, sticky enough to capture and retain the best talent at every juncture of a career.

Capture and keep her. It is not a finite window of success because older women have the benefit of resilience, entrepreneurism, *and* experience. They also add value as teachers and bring deep social networks. Failure to shift to a more holistic view of a woman's life and career is a missed opportunity to benefit from her skills and wisdom as she hits her true prime.

Offer a pathway back into the fold. Experiment with programs like "returnships" that offer skills training and opportunities to get back into the flow of a career and relaunch after an absence due to raising children, a partner's relocation, or elder caregiving.

Celebrate examples to inspire younger talent. The more that women in the earlier stages of their careers can be exposed to energetic older women being innovators, pioneers, trailblazers, and tycoons, the more they will see that the possible trajectory of their professional lives is limitless.

Develop age diversity. Make age part of your DE&I program. Beyond the diversity of perspectives that feeds innovation, older workers create a sense of "psychological safety" in the workplace, bringing wisdom and calm that can help foster greater productivity.

The book is still being written. Try not to get boxed into just one thing. The true trajectory of a professional life can take multiple twists and turns if you are open to new challenges. Think of your career as a page-turning series of chapters with some interesting subplots and a tantalizing surprise ending.

Epilogue

S o what's next? What can be done today, tomorrow, and in the months and years ahead to ensure that you, and the next generation of women leaders behind you, can take their long overdue place at the top table? It's all very well *knowing* that this is our moment to lead, with all the indisputable data points to prove it, but what matters most is how we *execute* upon that knowledge. How do we make sure that we seize this rare opportunity in history to build a population of senior women leaders who can influence and implement decisions that will not only result in a more representative workplace, but drive unprecedented economic success?

Thinking back to the many inspiring conversations I have had with women leaders while researching and writing this book, I am struck by the multitude of takeaways and actionable steps that individuals and organizations can take to move the needle forward on gender parity in the workplace. But the one throughline in all the stories they have shared is that we need to be bold. Whether you are an individual navigating your own career path to the top, or an organization's leader seeking to empower more women and underrepresented groups to do the same, you need to think in terms of leaps, not steps.

This is about revolution, not evolution, because the world cannot afford to wait. There needs to be a radical shift of mindset. It is time to reframe the concept of risk as a good thing, whether you are going for a more senior position and don't tick every single box on the job spec list, or you are part of a board expanding a CEO search beyond the usual suspects. You must give yourself permission to reach for it, even when no one else will.

When she was appointed president of a major record label, Julie Greenwald didn't wait for someone to greenlight her decision to populate more than half of her leadership team with women. More than two decades ago, before diversity, equity, and inclusion (DE&I) was even a thing, she was handed a "clean slate" to fill all the key positions and used the opportunity to recruit from a more diverse talent pool:

"You have to be forthright if you're going to create change and opportunity for women and minorities," Julie told me. "You have to actively make those decisions and not leave it to happenstance."

Marianne Bergmann Røren, CEO of Norwegian infrastructure company Mesta, looked nothing like the white male engineers who preceded her. But the company had been on a long downward spiral. A recruiter that Marianne was working with, who also happened to be a woman, convinced the board to look outside of the industry to find someone with a fresh perspective to help break the cycle of lackluster leadership and financial failure.

"Look, whatever you've been doing until now hasn't been working, so it's time to experiment," she told them.

Marianne continued expanding the talent pool for positions across her organization by pulling candidates from across sectors. "Yes, I took some chances, but that's what this new world is all about," Marianne told me.

The greater risk was not to experiment with diverse job candidates.

I can't think of two more different businesses, but both women were able to achieve major turnarounds with the same bold mindset. "We made some brave choices," Marianne said of Mesta's decision to go to 50–50. "But it worked."

As my RRA colleague Tina Shah Paikeday, our head of global capability for DE&I, suggests, it's time to prioritize potential. "There's been this narrative around women not being ready, but we have to do more hiring for potential if we actually want to see change at the top," Tina explained.

That requires systemic change to the recruitment process. Even when clients ask us to produce a diverse candidate list, the short list often seems to end up back where we started. Too often, women don't make it into these key roles because they haven't been given the opportunities to gain relevant operational experience as they have risen through the ranks. At the senior executive level they are usually chief marketing officers or chief people officers and haven't had the opportunity to oversee a P&L. Our data shows that there are far fewer women than men in the upper echelons with the most influential and powerful roles. For CEOs, that translates to 8.8% women, while 18% of CFOs are women, and 10% of COOs. Women make up only 20% of P&L leaders overall. By comparison, 67% of CHROs and 47% of CMOs are women.

This deplorable disparity helps to explain why senior women leaders have been leaving their companies en masse, according to an October 2022 report by McKinsey and LeanIn.org, which found that 15% more women quit their jobs the previous year than men, a much bigger differential than usual. Labeled the "Great Breakup," this report suggested that a major contributing factor to the resignations was the fact that many of these women had been passed up for promotions.

But these numbers are eminently fixable. Organizations need to be more intentional about giving women leaders more operational responsibilities earlier in their careers. We need more systems thinking combined with formal senior-level sponsorship to get us there, faster. Because, as evidenced by the stories you've read on the preceding pages, there's plenty of upside to the so-called risk of betting on a woman.

"To get the positive economic and business impact of having more diverse teams, you need to take that risk," Tina explained. "A deliberate and informed decision-making approach can lead to a much greater reward."

Research has also found that the more women at the top, the more diverse the leadership teams within the whole organization. According to Hypatia Capital, an asset management firm with a focus on women-led companies with diverse management teams, women hire women. Women CEOs have 164% more women in their executive leadership teams. These companies also tend to outperform, according to the Hypatia Women CEO Index. The few women who rise to these levels must, by definition, possess greater leadership skills than the average executives, who are mostly men, because those men did not face the same obstacles.[1]

So let's get tangible and actionable. What are some ways organizations can get more women into their companies' executive leadership roles and onto their board of directors – and create a more inclusive environment that women can thrive in?

First, although younger women want and need these changes, it is incumbent upon more established C-suite executives and board members to actually *make* these changes happen.

I've ended each chapter with a list of specific action steps for organizations and individuals to take to achieve parity. It's a combination of strategies, but with the onus on organizations to make some fundamental shifts in outlook and practices. Below is a distillation of these key takeaways, which will get us there in leaps and upward bounds:

- **Seize the opportunity in front of you.** Organizations (and their leaders) face a once-in-a-generation opportunity to accelerate progress towards parity and get more women at the top. It's not good enough to wait 130-plus years to close the equality gap. We need to do better now. And we can do better – for the benefit of business, women, and the world.

- **Walk the talk.** Build diversity targets into hiring decisions, and tether managers' hiring and retention successes to their bonuses. Make it a must-have, not a nice-to-have. And put your money where your mouth is by investing in more training and outreach to recruit and retain women.

- **Question your definitions of great leadership.** The leadership traits that worked in the past will not help your organization in the future. We all have ingrained unconscious biases: for example, is a lack of "gravitas" a fair criticism, or is she just not tall enough to match your expectations? Recognize that these biases exist – and how they hold you back.

- **Think outside the box.** Make bold hiring decisions to infuse your organization with more diversity. Be open to appointing or promoting people who do not check all the boxes. As Amy Bunszel, EVP of software giant Autodesk, said, "Position specifications are wish lists."

- **Remove biases.** Consider using blind resumes (which include no name, photos, or details about gender or race). They are a powerful way to overcome systemic biases and increase diversity across your upper management ranks. The famous "orchestra auditions" by Harvard University found blind interviews increased women auditioners' odds by 50%![2]

- **Build career paths that look like webs, not ladders.** Create an environment where people feel psychological safety if they need to walk, not run, for a few months or years in their personal career. Allow longer periods of time to reach milestone promotion marks. Just because they're not in the C-suite by the age of 50 doesn't mean it can't happen.

- **Foster inclusive meetings.** Don't start your board meeting with a round of golf, for example. (Did you know that the acronym GOLF stands for Guys Only, Ladies Forbidden?!) And maybe think of other activities besides hunting or fishing during your off-sites. The culture at the top needs to change so that senior women leaders can feel part of the conversation before they even get to the conference table.

- **Normalize extended paternity leave.** Parenting should be done by both men and women. It's not enough to have paternity leave options. You also need to create a culture in your organization where men feel no friction about taking that time with their families. Otherwise, you're sending the indirect message that "home and hearth" is up to women alone to manage.

- **Create "return to work" programs.** Timeouts shouldn't mean the end of careers. In fact, it pays to actively encourage time out (see Bain's Take Two program). Regardless of how much time away people have had, they still have plenty to contribute. Don't close the door to them.

- **Institutionalize sponsorship programs.** While women generally have a lot of mentors, they also need influential people who will champion them internally and externally. Match high-potential women with successful leaders (male and female) in your company.

And what about women themselves? What can *we* do to flip the odds of our success and power to get to the top of organizations? I began this book with a promise: you will not find on these pages a list of instructions on what to change within yourselves. And I meant that. I feel passionately that it is up to companies and their leaders to transform themselves (through the steps above, and much more). Where you have seen any takeaways for the individual, they have never been exhortations for you to change, because your authentic self is what has been missing in the top tiers of corporations. Rather, they have been calls to embrace all that you already are as a leader. Don't take a supportive role or allow yourself to be a "handmaiden" in a meeting. Figure out and demand your true financial worth. Take an entrepreneurial mindset – be bold and fearless, and remember you don't have to check every box before jumping in and founding a business idea. Extend your professional and personal support networks, reimagine your career arc, ditch that perfectionism. Set yourself up for the success you deserve by recognizing and trusting your intrinsic value and demanding that others to do the same. You owe it not only to yourself, but to the women who will be standing on your shoulders.

Your time has come.

Notes

Introduction

1. Gender Diversity in the C-suite, Russell Reynolds Associates, 2022.
2. Meera Jannathan, "There are more S&P 500 CEOs named Michael or James than women chief executives," December 10, 2020, https://www.marketwatch.com/story/there-are-more-s-p-500-ceos-named-michael-or-james-than-women-chief-executives-11607456463
3. "The Third Women's Revolution: Changing the World, with Arianna Huffington," https://bigthink.com/videos/the-third-womens-revolution/
4. Jack Zenger and Joseph Folkman, "Research: Women Are Better Leaders During a Crisis," December 30, 2020, https://hbr.org/2020/12/research-women-are-better-leaders-during-a-crisis
5. Greg Orme, "Women Leaders Have Shone During the Pandemic: Men, Take Note," August 4, 2021, https://www.forbes.com/sites/gregorme/2021/08/04/women-leaders-have-shone-during-the-pandemicambitious-men-should-take-note/?sh=564f550751c6
6. "Wisconsin School of Business, Leadership During the Pandemic: States with Women Governors Had Fewer COVID-19 Deaths," July 14, 2020, https://business.wisc.edu/news/leadership-during-the-pandemic-states-with-women-governors-had-fewer-covid-19-deaths/
7. World Economic Forum, "Global Gender Gap Report 2022," July 2022, https://www.weforum.org/reports/global-gender-gap-report-2022/
8. Lilly Singh, "'A Seat at the Table' Isn't the Solution for Gender Equity," https://www.youtube.com/watch?v=9EBkS2kE7uk

Chapter 1

1. Erika Engelhaupt, "How Do Women Deal With Having a Period... in Space?" https://www.nationalgeographic.co.uk/space/how-do-women-deal-with-having-a-period-in-space

2. Marcia Belsky, "That Time When NASA (Almost) Sent Sally Ride to Space with 100 Tampons," June 3, 2022, https://www.npr.org/transcripts/1102635355

3. Gender Diversity in the C-suite, Russell Reynolds Associates, 2022.

4. Richard V. Reeves and Ember Smith, "The Male College Crisis Is Not Just in Enrollment, But Completion," October 8, 2021, https://www.brookings.edu/blog/up-front/2021/10/08/the-male-college-crisis-is-not-just-in-enrollment-but-completion/

5. Kevin Sneader and Lareina Yee, "Confronting the Early-Career Gender Gap," January 9, 2020, https://www.mckinsey.com/business-functions/people-and-organizational-performance/our-insights/confronting-the-early-career-gender-gap

6. Cecilia Kang and Erin Griffith, "What Sheryl Sandberg's Exit Reveals About Women's Progress," June 3, 2022, https://www.nytimes.com/2022/06/03/technology/sheryl-sandberg-women-in-tech.html

7. "Fewer Women Than Men Will Regain Employment During the COVID-19 Recovery Says ILO," July 19, 2021, https://www.ilo.org/global/about-the-ilo/newsroom/news/WCMS_813449/lang—en/index.htm

8. Russell Reynolds Associates, "Why Is Everybody Leaving? 8 Equitable Steps to Retain Your Diverse Talent," https://www.russellreynolds.com/en/insights/articles/why-is-everybody-leaving

9. Russell Reynolds Associates, "Why Is Everybody Leaving? 8 Equitable Steps to Retain Your Diverse Talent," https://www.russellreynolds.com/en/insights/articles/why-is-everybody-leaving

10. Divides and Dividends, Russell Reynolds Associates, 2021, https://www.russellreynolds.com/en/insights/divides-and-dividends

11. Stewart D. Friedman, "Be a Better Leader, Have a Richer Life," April 2008, https://hbr.org/2008/04/be-a-better-leader-have-a-richer-life

12. Stewart Friedman, "'Having It All' Is Not a Women's Issue," June 26, 2012, https://hbr.org/2012/06/having-it-all-is-not-a-womens

Chapter 2

1. "Hedy Lamarr, Engineer," March 6, 2018, http://www.theheroinecollective.com/hedy-lamarr/

2. Phil Wahba, "A Record 12,200 U.S. Stores Closed in 2020 as E-commerce, Pandemic Changed Retail Forever," January 7, 2021, https://fortune.com/2021/01/07/record-store-closings-bankruptcy-2020/

3. Melissa Repko, "Ulta Beauty CEO Says Retailers Need Support from Washington: 'We Need Companies to Survive,'" March 25, 2020, https://www.cnbc.com/2020/03/25/ulta-beauty-ceo-says-retailers-need-support-from-washington-we-need-companies-to-survive.html

4. Aneel Chima and Ron Gutman, "What It Takes to Lead Through an Era of Exponential Change," October 2020, https://hbr.org/2020/10/what-it-takes-to-lead-through-an-era-of-exponential-change#:~:text=Leader%20humility%2C%20authenticity%2C%20and%20openness,effectively%20navigating%203%2DD%20change

5. Phil Wahba, "A Record 12,200 U.S. Stores Closed in 2020 as E-commerce, Pandemic Changed Retail Forever," January 7, 2021, https://hbr.org/2020/10/what-it-takes-to-lead-through-an-era-of-exponential-change?ab=at_art_art_1x4_s04

6. Aneel Chima and Ron Gutman, "What It Takes to Lead Through an Era of Exponential Change," October 29, 2020, https://hbr.org/2020/10/what-it-takes-to-lead-through-an-era-of-exponential-change?ab=at_art_art_1x4_s04

Chapter 3

1. "Moving Beyond Remote: Workplace Transformation in the Wake of Covid-19," October 7, 2020, https://slack.com/blog/collaboration/workplace-transformation-in-the-wake-of-covid-19

2. "One Year into the Pandemic: ADP Research Institute® Uncovers How Working Conditions and Attitudes Have Changed in Global

Study," April 28, 2021, https://mediacenter.adp.com/2021-04-28-One-Year-into-the-Pandemic-ADP-Research-Institute-R-Uncovers-How-Working-Conditions-and-Attitudes-Have-Changed-in-Global-Study

3. "State of Remote Work, 2021," https://owllabs.com/state-of-remote-work/2021/

4. "10 Quotes from Susan Cain's Quiet to Inspire Introverted Architects," July 13, 2019, https://blog.archisnapper.com/10-quotes-from-susan-cains-quiet-to-inspire-introverted-architects/

5. Deanna Cuadra, "Make Self-Care a Priority: A Look at Zendesk's Well-Being Benefits," December 8, 2021, https://www.benefitnews.com/news/zendesk-explores-its-well-being-benefits-for-mental-health

6. Anna Codrea-Rado, "Can Slack Improve Workplace Culture for Women?" February 7, 2018, https://www.dell.com/en-uk/perspectives/can-slack-improve-workplace-culture-for-women/

7. How To Lead Inclusive Meetings, https://www.forbes.com/sites/rebekahbastian/2019/05/28/how-to-lead-inclusive-meetings/?sh=d351d77ffede.

8. "What's Next for Remote Work: An Analysis of 2,000 Tasks, 800 Jobs, and Nine Countries," November 23, 2020, https://www.mckinsey.com/featured-insights/future-of-work/whats-next-for-remote-work-an-analysis-of-2000-tasks-800-jobs-and-nine-countries

Chapter 4

1. Russell Reynolds Associates, "Power, Politics and Purpose: Leadership Lessons with Former PM of Australia Julia Gillard," Redefiners podcast, season 2, episode 7, https://www.russellreynolds.com/en/insights/podcasts/leadership-lessons-with-former-pm-of-australia-julia-gillard

2. Tonja Jacobi and Dylan Schweers, "Female Supreme Court Justices Are Interrupted More by Male Justices and Advocates," April 11,

2017, https://hbr.org/2017/04/female-supreme-court-justices-are-interrupted-more-by-male-justices-and-advocates

3. McKinsey & Company, "Dame Vivian Hunt," https://www.mckinsey.com/our-people/vivian-hunt

Chapter 5

1. Paola Peralta, "Glassdoor Reveals Why Women Aren't Asking for Pay Raises," April 7, 2021, https://www.benefitnews.com/news/why-women-dont-know-how-to-ask-for-a-pay-raise

2. Ibid.

3. Melissa Korn, Lauren Weber, and Andrea Fuller, "Data Show Gender Pay Gap Opens Early," August 8, 2022, https://www.wsj.com/articles/gender-pay-gap-college-11659968901?mod=djemwhatsnews

Chapter 6

1. Gretchen Livingston and Deja Thomas, "Among 41 Countries, Only U.S. Lacks Paid Parental Leave," December 16, 2019, https://www.pewresearch.org/fact-tank/2019/12/16/u-s-lacks-mandated-paid-parental-leave/

2. Eight ways the world is not designed for women - BBC News. https://www.bbc.co.uk/news/world-us-canada-47725946

Chapter 7

1. Katie Abel, "Exclusive: Nike's New North America Head Sarah Mensah on Being a 'Real and Present' Leader and What She Learned from Michael Jordan," May 14, 2021, https://footwearnews.com/2021/business/power-players/nike-sarah-mensah-leadership-career-advice-1203140053/

2. Katie Abel, "Sarah Mensah on Being the First Black Woman to Head Up Nike North America," May 16, 2022, https://footwearnews .com/2022/business/power-players/nike-sarah-mensah-black-female-executive-north-america-1203287035/

3. Hubert Joly, "Former Best Buy Chief Hubert Joly's 10 Keys to CEO Transition," https://chiefexecutive.net/is-your-company-ready-to-make-a-ceo-transition-here-are-the-10-keys-to-success/

4. Brian Uzzi, "Research: Men and Women Need Different Kinds of Networks to Succeed," February 25, 2019, https://hbr.org/2019/02/research-men-and-women-need-different-kinds-of-networks-to-succeed

5. Lizette Chapman, "Female Founders Raised Just 2% of Venture Capital Money in 2021," January 11, 2022, https://www.bloomberg .com/news/articles/2022-01-11/women-founders-raised-just-2-of-venture-capital-money-last-year

6. "Why Women on Boards? Research Studies Point to the Value Women Bring to Boards," https://www.womensleadershipfoundation .org/why-women-on-boards

7. Julia Dawson, Richard Kersley, and Stefano Natella, "The CS Gender 3000: The Reward for Change," September 2016, https://static1.squarespace.com/static/5d4dc6663c80a1000100b072/t/5e97b501bc1186542410bfe9/1587000597468/CS+Gender+3000+2016.pdf

8. Rebecca Cassells and Alan Duncan, "Gender Equity Insights 2021: Making It a Priority," Bankwest Curtin Economics Centre Report, Gender Equity Series 6, March 2021, chrome-extension://efaidnbmnnnibpcajpcglclefindmkaj/https://www.wgea.gov.au/sites/default/files/documents/BCEC%20WGEA%20Gender%20Equity%20Insights%202021%20Report.pdf

9. "Why Women on Boards?"

Chapter 8

1. Forbes Asia, "Asia's Power Businesswomen," November 30, 2021, https://www.forbes.com/sites/ranawehbe/2021/11/01/asias-power-businesswomen-2021/?sh=2b1b0d357c29

2. "Women Are More Productive Then Men, According to New Research," October 8, 2018, https://www.weforum.org/agenda/2018/10/women-are-more-productive-than-men-at-work-these-days#:~:text=Who%20produces%20more%2C%20men%20or,percent%20of%20their%20assigned%20work

3. RRA Proprietary Analysis, S&P100 Leadership Teams, 2022 (n=100 companies, 1583 executives).

4. Olivia Rockeman, "The Mystery of the Missing Workers, Explained," August 5, 2021, https://www.bloomberg.com/news/features/2021-08-05/why-is-u-s-labor-force-shrinking-retirement-boom-opioid-crisis-child-care

5. Aliza Knox, "Ageism Is Old Fashioned: Why You Should Nurture Older Executives," June 21, 2021, https://www.forbes.com/sites/alizaknox/2021/06/21/ageism-is-old-fashioned-why-you-should-nurture-older-executives/?sh=1e4c962d9f90

6. Josh Bersin, and, Tomas Chamorro-Premuzic, "The Case for Hiring Older Workers," September 26, 2019, https://hbr.org/2019/09/the-case-for-hiring-older-workers

7. Maggie McGrath, "Introducing the 50 Over 50: Women Proving Success Has No Age Limit," June 2, 2021, https://www.forbes.com/sites/maggiemcgrath/2021/06/02/introducing-the-50-over-50-women-proving-success-has-no-age-limit/?sh=7cd2aed45b40

8. *Redline* magazine, October 2022, https://www.redonline.co.uk

9. Nye Cominetti, "A U-Shaped Crisis: The Impact of the Covid-19 Crisis on Older Workers," April 26, 2021, https://www.resolutionfoundation.org/publications/a-u-shaped-crisis/

10. Aliza Knox, "Ageism Is Old Fashioned: Why You Should Nurture Older Executives," June 21, 2021, https://www.forbes.com/sites/alizaknox/2021/06/21/ageism-is-old-fashioned-why-you-should-nurture-older-executives/?sh=1e4c962d9f90
11. "Cognizant Returnship® Program," https://careers.cognizant.com/global/en/cognizant-returnship-program
12. Bill Snyder, "How Mindy Grossman Turned Around HSN," June 5, 2014, https://www.gsb.stanford.edu/insights/how-mindy-grossman-turned-around-hsn
13. Sumiko Tan, "Lunch with Sumiko: It's a family affair at EtonHouse group of schools as son helps mum to oversee business," April 24, 2022, https://www.straitstimes.com/singapore/parenting-education/lunch-with-sumiko-so-far-so-good-very-blessed

Epilogue

1. Hypatia Women Ceo Index Fact Sheet, https://www.wilshire.com/resources-and-forms/hypatia-women-ceo-index-fact-sheet
2. NBER, Orchestrating Impartiality: The Impact of "Blind" Auditions on Female Musicians, https://www.nber.org/papers/w5903.

Index